For information visit: www.writeranne.net
Cover art: Annette Hassell www.annettehassell.com
Cover design, wolf icon design, and chart recreation: Beezley Design Studio www.trisbeezley.com

ISBN: 978-0-9984286-2-8 (print)
First Edition: October 2019

Porter

Dedication

For Susan, my soul sister, without whom there wouldn't be a story.

For Colin, Jelena, and JC, who, along with Susan, have made me part of their family and lovingly shared their home and lives with me and Andrew during this process.

For Tom Jenkins, who never gave up on me and cheered me on so many times in my struggle to become a writer.

And for Porter of course—my Wolfie. My boy.

For Mic,

Enjoy! All the best!

Anne

AE

Special Thanks

This is the first book I've written that is not mine. It belongs to Porter, of course, and I'm infinitely grateful for the gift of his love and presence in my experience, and for all that I continue to learn from him. It belongs to all of Porter's people (you know who you are). It belongs to Colin, JC and Jelena, and for them there will never be enough thanks—for opening their hearts and home to me for the past year, and most of all for the precious gift of their friendship. But more than anyone else, this book belongs to Susan, who birthed it right along with me—I will never be able to thank her for all that she has done as my production partner and my friend to bring this project to fruition.

Thank you to everyone who allowed me to interview them (sometimes multiple times), including Megan Hickman and Cheyenne DeBoard.

I can't thank my beta readers enough for their patience and dedication to this project and for helping me make this book the best it could be: Susan, Colin, Dan, Renee, Sara, Gayle and Andrew.

Thank you to my chosen mentors, Renee Ashley, Bunny McBride, and, unbeknownst to her, Elizabeth Gilbert.

A book doesn't get published in a vacuum, and I will be forever indebted to my creative Dream Team: my editor Elizabeth Cameron, the cover artist and dear friend Annette Hassell, my graphic designer, also a dear friend, Tris Beezley, and Jeff Thacher for his extraordinary talent in producing the book trailer.

And thank you to my husband and partner in all things, without whom I could not live the life I do. Success is all the sweeter because I can share it with him.

Foreword

Porter's story has so many elements and layers: it is one of educating the public that he isn't at all a "big bad wolf"; it is one of overcoming anxiety and fear (he was a 120-pound abused and unsocialized wolfdog, afraid of us, untrusting of us and protective of himself); it is one of transforming fear into understanding and anxiety into love, which is really a great analogy for life in general; it is one of jumping right in to do what's right regardless of how it will end up; it is one of both Porter and me overcoming obstacles; and it is one of knowledge—I had to learn wolf behaviors and he had to learn his place in society through special training, without which we couldn't have kept him. It is a story of "stick-to-it-iveness"—we never gave up on each other. But the greatest story of all, and Porter's real purpose, lies in people, all the people we met who have become important to us because of Porter—from the vet who gave him a second chance to neighbors and friends we made on walks, and people he brought back into our lives, like the author and her husband.

Why should Porter's story be told? Because it should have ended almost six years ago when he was chained up in a muddy back yard, left behind as an inconvenience. The vet that was called to end his life instead gave him a new lease on life, and that's where the story begins. What came next was trust, growth, love, friendships, and a world far wider than that afforded him on a thirty-foot chain.

Ever since Porter came into our lives and I started posting his photos, Anne's sweetness toward him was evidenced in her comments and I was touched by her gentleness and honesty. I was led to make a comment of my own on her author page suggesting that she write his story. Even though I don't think I knew there was a story, or at least enough of a story, at the time, I was compelled to post those few words—I can't really describe it other than that. If his story is to be told, it needs to be told by someone with an understanding heart. That is Anne Eston.

– Susan, Porter's owner

Author's Note

Several people have asked both Susan and me, "Why this story? What makes this story more important or special than any other rescue story?" It would be easy to point out that no story is ever completely new. Every story has hints and shades of other stories that have come before it. But to offer such a response is, like the question itself, a futile engagement in comparison. It is also incomplete.

The most important part of Porter's story is neither the horror of the circumstances that led to his rescue nor the mere report of his wellbeing since Susan adopted him. It is all that has transpired since his rescue that makes for a story worth telling.

As Susan has said to me, Porter's story is really one of people—all those whose lives he has touched directly and indirectly as his own life has expanded so far beyond the thirty-foot chain on which he was kept for the first six years of it.

Porter is also an ambassador for his breed—one to be respected rather than feared. And his story is an example of how much is truly required of a wolfdog owner, and what an amazing experience it can be for both the owner and the animal when the responsibility is taken seriously.

For these reasons, Susan called upon me to write Porter's

story, and I accepted the call. I've also thought about my own reasons for writing this story. As the author, I am both Porter's biographer and the storyteller of my own experience of being gifted with his affection and acceptance. I am also, in a sense, Porter's voice. This has been an exercise in balancing an unfiltered account of all that Porter and Susan and her family have had to overcome together with my own unapologetic affection for him. The result has been to offer an intelligent framework for the challenges Porter and his humans have overcome, not through rose-colored lenses, but with the perspective of the growth and intelligence he has demonstrated—all that he has become and shown himself to be since he was rescued.

As such, this is not a reference guide to the breed (although, thanks to the input of some experts, I have compiled a resource list for further reading and research at the back of the book), nor is it a commentary on the propagation of the breed. It is one story of one wolfdog, his rescue, and his impact on the lives around him.

Elizabeth Gilbert writes in what she jokingly refers to as her Free 10-Step Writing School to "Tell your story TO someone. Pick one person you love or admire or want to connect with and write the whole thing directly to them—like you're writing a letter." I did have a muse that I chose to write to during the arduous revision process. And of course, I consider this book to be my love letter to Porter. But now I invite you, the reader, to pull up a chair and get to know this magnificent boy and his story.

– Anne Eston

Additional Notes

This story is not told chronologically, with the exception of the rescue, which is the inevitable beginning. Consequently, some facts and events appear more than once in different contexts.

Most surnames have been omitted in order to protect individual privacy.

A portion of the proceeds from every sale will be donated to one or more wolf sanctuaries or foundations of the author's choosing.

The Rescue

"One always begins to forgive a place as soon as it's left behind."
– Charles Dickens

I often change the channel when the networks run the ASPCA ads at Christmastime with Sarah McLachlan singing in the background. I don't click on the articles in my newsfeed about animal abuse, culling, killing and poaching, slaughterhouses, or the suffering of animals. Not because I don't care, but because the images and videos are simply too much for me. This is probably why I didn't want to look at the first photos of Porter chained in the muddy yard in his former home. Didn't want to imagine, as I looked into his eyes, how he'd been struck on the head to discipline him or maybe just out of meanness. Didn't want to imagine him alone after his former owner moved away and abandoned him.

But I had to, for the sake of the story. And for Porter. If any vestige of his former life remains in Porter's memory, we can hope that its lasting effect on him will fade, if not be forgotten or forgiven.

Piecing together the details of the rescue proved to be a challenge for all concerned. No formal record remains of his rescue, neither with the mobile vet nor with his new owners Susan and her husband. No one could have known at the time that there would ever be a reason to recall these events or to revisit them in any detail.

The circumstances of Porter's life before Susan adopted him are memories that serve as reminders of all that he has survived and overcome at best, and that provoke sadness and questions—all of which begin with "Why?"—at worst.

Upon looking at current Google images of the house (which were obtained by a legal Internet search of the address using the former owner's name, of which Susan was in possession), Susan is almost incredulous. "It doesn't look anything like what I remember," she says of the day she and her husband Colin went to see Porter. "It was a dark, blustery Ohio day with a driving, icy rain—thoroughly miserable. The house behind which Porter lived disappeared into the gray day as unmemorable and bleak. There was a heaviness in everything we saw."

I drove there myself on a warm autumn day not long before this book was published. The surrounding neighborhood was pleasant enough, with houses of various sizes, mostly well-kept. But when I turned down the narrow street where the house is, a normally innocuous "No Outlet" sign marks the entrance, and the road itself is in almost complete disrepair, with multiple potholes and deeply cracked pavement. There was an unusual number of cars in the driveways of the neighboring houses for a weekday afternoon as I approached the one where Porter's former owner (we'll call him "Ted") lived. Not wanting to raise suspicion by stopping or getting out, I passed slowly by, turned around at the end of the street and passed again on my way back to the main road from which I turned in. I could see from the road that the land in the back of the house dipped and was thick with overgrown foliage. The house itself appeared to be inhabited, but the garage behind it was worn and dilapidated. I wondered who had lived there since Ted, and if that same individual or family lived there now. When I drove away, I didn't regret going to see the house for myself, but like Susan and Colin, I never need to see it again. Later I told Susan about my pilgrimage, and that I'd passed Mt. Airy Forest on my way back to the highway. To my horror, she told me that Ted had said that more than once, Porter had gotten loose, ran to the forest dragging the chain, and had snagged himself. He'd then howl until Ted heard him and would come to untangled him from whatever his chain had gotten snagged on. He'd bring Porter back—only to re-secure him on the chain in the back yard. This

11

knowledge only made me more grateful that Porter was finally free of that chain.

But before Susan and Colin ever became involved in Porter's rescue, Ted made a phone call to Mike's Mobile Vet, which put the rescue in motion, but with a very different outcome in mind.

Mike's wife, and partner in the mobile veterinary service, Eleni, took the call, on a rainy day in early December of 2013. "I was shocked when Porter's owner called our office requesting to euthanize him. I said I would have to check with Mike to see if he would agree to do that because our policy is that we don't euthanize healthy pets. I asked Ted the usual list of questions that I ask any new client, including whether or not the animal is sick and how old it is. I was essentially searching for a reason why he was giving up on his dog." As far she knows, Ted didn't make any effort to re-home Porter before calling them. Ted was moving away, and his new house didn't have a yard big enough; he also didn't feel that he had enough time to care for Porter. These are the reasons he gave to Eleni for requesting that she and Mike come to dispose of him.

"I called Ted back after Mike adamantly refused to euthanize Porter and asked him for more time to find a solution—we needed Ted to give us time. We wanted the best option for Porter to get a better life. Porter's dire need was our motivation to work with the owner as much as possible," says Eleni. Thankfully he agreed. "As easy as it is to blame Ted for giving up because his lifestyle had changed, he did care enough to give us that time. I believe Ted was willing to work with us because we responded with love."

After that initial phone call, Eleni stayed in daily contact with Ted by phone to reassure him that she and Mike were doing everything humanly possible to find a home for Porter. She also made daily calls to rescues across the country to find help.

Unfortunately, rescue operations and wolf sanctuaries were unable to take Porter for several reasons. Eleni says cost, difficulty integrating intact males into a group of other dogs, and Porter's lack of socialization were the reasons she was not able to place him in a rescue or sanctuary.

As a last resort, Eleni created a Facebook post. She and Susan had been friends through their church and were already connected on Facebook, which is how Susan saw the post. Susan and Colin had owned a wolfdog before and thought that they understood what was involved in raising one, but nothing prepared them for what rescuing Porter would require.

"I saw this magnificent animal on Eleni's post, both his

puppy photo and current photos, and read about the dire situation. I immediately thought 'we must help!'" The post said he was kid-friendly and dog- and cat-friendly, only one of which would turn out to be true, unbeknownst to Susan at the time.

So Eleni arranged for her and Mike to accompany Susan and Colin to Ted's house to see Porter. What they found was dismal:

"Porter was muddy and he was drenched," says Susan. "I didn't know about his impeccable grooming habits then. But in hindsight, it had to be frustrating for him not to be able to keep himself clean. But more than that, the conditions he lived in were abysmal and the chain meant he could only move so far in any direction. The yard was sloppy and there was a busted fence that was supposed to serve as a secondary containment if Porter ever were to break free of the chain. The thought of him being alone every day in that setting weighed heavily on me."

"Porter's fenced-in area was some distance from the house. It was muddy, with no grass, and a single tree next to a dilapidated doghouse," Eleni confirms. "The fence was in desperate need of repair, so Porter was chained around the clock so that he wouldn't escape."

Susan goes on to describe their first encounter with Ted and Porter that day. "Ted met us all at the house. Porter seemed

14

skittish even of him and would start to approach us while still on his chain and then dart back in fear. He was afraid of all of us and not even warm with Ted," she says. "I remember being in awe and half in love with his beauty, but also a bit nervous, because he didn't appear friendly. I realize now that he was just scared. He wasn't the adorable puppy someone immediately falls in love with. But he was beautiful—and scary, filthy, sad, and lonely."

Mike and Eleni's first impression of Porter and that scene reflects their perspective as veterinary professionals. Mike experienced Ted as quiet. Eleni describes him as a family man, and although she and Mike never met his wife and children, she had the impression that he was moving to better their lives. She also had the impression that Ted's wife hadn't given him much of a choice regarding the move, or Porter.

"When we actually saw Porter, we felt compassion for him and for Ted. Unfortunately, in our line of work, we see the difficult, more emotional cases. We aren't immune, but in Porter's circumstance, we were as gracious as we possibly could be in the face of the rain, mud, dilapidated house, broken fence, and his heavy chain. When Ted eventually brought him out from his area that day, he said that was the first time Porter was on grass in days, or possibly weeks."

"We all went to the back with Ted," continues Susan.

"None of us went in his fenced yard or within the radius of the reach of his chain. Colin and I were at the fence opening and Porter was terrified. His tail was tucked far between his legs. I remember being intimidated. Ted went back to the house to get Porter's collar and leash, and then he stepped into the fenced area with Porter. We stood alone at the fence for a few moments and didn't know what to think. Porter didn't seem comfortable with Ted either, who then leashed Porter up and brought him to the front yard where it wasn't as sloppy. I remember walking Porter down the street. He pulled and was hard to control, which was also intimidating for me. We were willing to take him that day, but Porter wouldn't get into our car. We tried to get him to go with us, but he was terrified."

According to Ted, Porter was a gift from his brother and had been between two and three months old when Ted got him. Porter came from a breeder in the South, and it's thought to be one in Tennessee. He had told Eleni Porter was a game dog, meaning that Porter would kill and eat whatever birds, raccoons, and squirrels wandered into his radius on the thirty-foot chain. Susan remembers Ted telling her that he only came back to the house after he moved every other day or so to feed Porter.

Ted and his brother had considered becoming breeders. They soon discovered all the difficulties that were involved, but this is probably the reason that Porter remained unneutered until Susan and Colin adopted him.

Susan also experienced the challenges of caring for a six-year-old intact unsocialized male wolfdog during a period when she and Colin questioned whether or not they were the right people to care for Porter. At least one wolf sanctuary told her that wolfdogs are less predictable than full-blooded wolves, as well as too domesticated and asocial, according to what Eleni encountered, and for these reasons, wolf sanctuaries and rescues are unlikely to take them in.

When Susan first approached Colin about possibly adopting Porter, his response was that he would not stand in the way of anything that she thought was the right thing to do. When I asked what sealed the decision to adopt him, Susan said that while Porter didn't look much like Sayan, another dog they had years before, his former owner claimed that he was a wolfdog. "DNA technology is recent, so content was guessed in those days," says Susan. "If he had wolf content, it was low."

Colin confirms, "Having Sayan is a big reason why we considered accepting Porter in the first place." Susan and Colin had Sayan for four or five years. While they did see evidence of a strong prey drive (he did kill a rabbit and a cat during his time with Susan and Colin, but unlike Porter, Sayan didn't eat the rabbit), Susan describes him as "a big lover" with mostly dog behaviors. She adds that he was big enough for her three-year-old son at the time to climb on and hug, but that he was really no different than their other family pets. While Sayan was originally named for a mountain range in southern Siberia, it's also interesting to note the Hindu origin and meanings of the name, which include "kind heart," "precious friend," and "companion," according to two online name-origin sites. Susan says "Despite his prey drive, it was because of Sayan's big heart that we felt we could handle Porter. But we didn't realize how different Porter would be."

Susan and Colin decided they would take Porter, and it was agreed that Ted would bring Porter to their home the next afternoon, three days before Christmas, at two o'clock. But the next day, as Colin and Susan thought the situation through, they were having second thoughts. They had young children and other pets to consider and wondered if they were being irresponsible in this decision. But before they could call to tell Ted that they had changed their minds, Ted arrived two hours early with Porter and left him there with just the chain he had lived on for six years.

Even if we were able to speak to Ted today, it might be difficult to reconcile the man who wanted the best for his family with the irresponsible owner of a wolfdog who, out of some combination of ignorance and lack of humanity, mistreated Porter the way he did. It would be months before Susan and Colin could touch Porter on the top of his head, since he showed obvious signs of having been hit there out of discipline, and longer still before specialized training would allow him to enjoy the life of walks with them and their other properly socialized dogs.

But to keep looking for the "why" in these situations is rarely beneficial, and tends to keep all involved rooted in a horrific past.

As Ted disappeared down Susan and Colin's driveway, leaving Porter there with nothing but a thirty-foot chain, their adventure as new owners and caregivers of a six-year-old unsocialized wolfdog—and Porter's new life—had begun.

Caring for a Wolfdog

Just as every dog is different, every wolfdog is different. Not only do they require proper space and exercise, but the age of the wolfdog when it's adopted, what type of responsible early training is offered, and certainly wolf content can play a role in building trust from an early age, and in the overall health of the animal–owner relationship. In addition to these elements, patience, education, and time are also huge factors in the successful integration of the animal.

The community of wolfdog owners can be a great source of support and information, but it can also be mired in judgment about what's best for one's own animal. Susan has experienced the gamut of feedback from other wolfdog owners on social media, from ardent support to snap judgments about her choices in caring for Porter without understanding the requirements of his unique situation. But the resources listed in the back are excellent places for information about what it takes to properly and responsibly care for a wolfdog, and have proven to be invaluable to Susan over the years.

Space

One of the first things Susan and Colin learned was that Porter not only loves being outdoors (he thrives during the winter months, when his thick coat protects him in all but the most bitter of temperatures), but that being indoors actually causes him a good deal of stress.

On one of Porter's first nights with them, Colin had thought he would be fine to stay in a room off of the basement. He and Susan heard noises but didn't think anything of it at first, until the sounds escalated. When they went to check, Porter had ripped the doorframe off, along with the crank handle on the window. He did not want to be inside and was determined to get out!

While it's unlikely that he will ever be a house pet, he has recently become more comfortable indoors for short periods of time, and during the heat of summer has been able to relax in his indoor kennel in the comfort of air conditioning.

Because Porter was an outdoor animal, Colin and Susan had to find the right solution for him. Porter came to them with only the chain he'd been kept on. While he does get along with their other two dogs, Sweetie and Scout, he didn't at first, and it wasn't entirely safe or practical to keep him in the same outdoor

22

enclosure with them—not only could he easily jump the fencing or dig under it, but even in play he would escalate to an uncomfortable level for their safety, so all of their interactions needed be closely monitored. They quickly realized this meant that they would have to build Porter his own enclosure.

It was several months before Susan and Colin were able to move forward with this project, as it was a significant financial commitment. In the interim, Porter was still on the chain, and was provided hay for bedding on their lawn, a big step up from the muddy lot he was kept in before. And, of course, he was amply fed and given fresh water, never left to fend for himself again.

"It struck me that Porter's life really started when he got off the chain for the first time," says Susan. "I remember Porter's trainer, Fred, saying how important it was to get him off the chain and build his enclosure. The chain was frustrating for him. He could go thirty feet this way or that, but his whole world was in that circumference. It makes an animal protective of all they have, especially their food, and it makes them aggressive. But more importantly, once he got off the chain, his world and experiences expanded, and he found his people—all of them!"

As soon as the weather cooperated, Susan called on one of her dearest and most trusted friends to tackle the job: Dale

23

Eads of Eads Fence.

"We built a heavy-duty chain-link enclosure, and approximately twenty by fifteen by ten feet, a foot deep into the ground, then buried the chain-link fence in the trench," explains Dale. "We installed a rail on the bottom to make the bottom more rigid. This setup prevents Porter from potentially climbing and getting out of the top or digging out through the bottom." He also added a three-foot dig guard (this is laid horizontally underground) around the circumference of the enclosure to prevent Porter from digging out of his enclosure.

As the owner of Eads Fence, Dale had built miles of dog fencing, but had never built one of this magnitude. It was actually his experience with building animal-containment fences for other species that helped him to be successful in designing Porter's enclosure.

"I have built enclosures for tropical birds, raccoons, rabbits, monkeys, lions, panthers, cheetahs, alligators, camels, ostriches, emus, zebras, buffalo, and rhinos." Dale's clients have included the Cincinnati Zoo, where Eads Fence built the cheetah enclosure, and the Newport Aquarium in Kentucky, where the company built the Mighty Mike alligator display. "I understood how strong and durable this enclosure needed to be. The enclosure took approximately seven to nine days to build."

Exercise

When speaking of the other pets they've had, Colin recalls a dog that had an issue with excessive barking. "He needed more interaction, and more exercise. I now know that he required more like what we do for Porter—more exercise and together time with him." He adds that having Porter has meant more walks with Susan and their other dogs that he wouldn't otherwise have had. "These are all lessons we're learning just because of Porter."

As a distance runner, exercising Porter is natural for Susan. She walks Porter an average of six miles per day, split between a morning and an evening walk in all but the most severe weather. These walks not only provide the exercise and mental stimulation he needs, but they also serve to build trust and respect between them both.

Diet

In the beginning, Porter's trainer, Fred Russell, was Susan's source in deciding what to feed him and how often. He suggested raw meat once or twice a week combined with high-quality kibble twice daily. Others in the community of wolfdog owners share similar practices on social media.

"Our dog food has always been high quality from PetPeople, and so have our treats—no grocery-store brands," explains Susan. "We started feeding him Blue Buffalo after we were so impressed with the grant we got from them when Porter was diagnosed a fourth time with cancer. That money helped tremendously to offset the cost of the needed surgery and radiation treatment [that followed]."

Due to more recent digestive challenges, Susan has had to rely on a specific prescription diet and forgo some of Porter's favorite treats, such as raw meat and bones. He also tends to grab up random things on walks, like roadkill, trash, etc., probably because he wasn't regularly fed at times by his former owner and had to survive on what he could find within the radius of his chain. "Porter loves eating anything that smells tasty," Susan says. "This remains an even greater challenge now that he is on a prescription diet, and I need to be more vigilant than ever."

Grooming

It's easy to assume that Porter's thick coat would require frequent brushing, similar to other breeds like huskies, Malamutes, and Samoyeds. But in fact, Porter will not allow Susan or anyone to groom him. And that's okay, because, as Susan says, he's fastidious with his grooming, just like a cat. And while he wasn't able to maintain that level of cleanliness living chained in muddy conditions, Susan says, "The first day we had him, you never would have known he was living in filth. He groomed himself once he had a clean, dry, warm area to do so."

The Education of Porter—and His People

"Every dog I work with teaches me something, and the more you work with them, the more they show you what they need and how they need it." – Fred Russell, Porter's Trainer

Off the Chain

It wasn't too long after Susan adopted Porter that she realized that she would need the support of a specialized trainer. She was fortunate enough to find Fred Russell.

Not every method of training is suitable for every dog, especially a wolfdog. Fred employs a combination of American Standard (based on the Schutzhund training method, which has three concentrations, according to the United Schutzhund Clubs of America: tracking, obedience, and protection) and the Volhard method, a softer 4H style that's not as rigid and tends to be better for shy or skittish animals. He chooses a mixture that fits the person and the dog. "You have to read the animal and also the people to get the method that's best suited for them," he says. While he speaks highly of popular trainers like César Millán, he doesn't put much stock in the methods of the large chain pet stores, mainly because their staff often isn't properly trained or certified in dog training.

Sometimes that means being tough, but "people don't pay me not to get the job done," he says. "If you don't stand up, that dog's going to know it. Whether it's a wolfdog or a chihuahua. I'm tough on certain things and you might not understand it in the beginning, but you'll see it in the end result. I do it on purpose. I've got to put you in the worst scenario and bring you out of it without anybody getting hurt. When you see how you've changed the dog's mind, you've educated the dog and communicated that 'I'm the pack leader, I'm the alpha, so I've got to teach him what I need him to understand.'"

Fred has worked with a variety of dogs in his thirty-eight years as a trainer. He took a German shepherd in the kennel of a K-9 security company that no one wanted to work with and turned the situation around. "Something struck me with this one dog," says Fred. "Nobody messed with him. He'd jumped on a couple of the handlers. So the head of the business gave me permission to work with him. When I got him out they were all watching me in the windows. I gave him a correction and we went on and afterward they told me that any handler that had given him a correction, he'd jumped on them. So I just kept on working with him, taking him out, doing things with him. I told the groomers not to handle him, that I'd put him on my schedule and feed him too. I got him healthy and active. I was there on a temporary assignment, and he was still there when I left."

"Fred's ability to work with animals that other handlers can't is remarkable," says Susan. "There seems to be an unspoken communication between him and the animal in training that has an immediate calming effect. Colin and I witnessed this on Fred's very first visit to meet Porter."

Most of Fred's clients come to him by word of mouth. An employee at a local coffee shop connected Fred with Patti, the owner of a Belgian Malinois–Dutch shepherd mix named Nikki, who had been formally trained but was afraid of daylight and to be out in the daytime. Fred visited Patti at her home, and while they talked, Fred wondered why he hadn't seen any sign of Nikki, especially since she was trained to be a protection dog. "I asked her where the dog was, and Nikki was downstairs in the kennel. Patti got a leash but Nikki didn't want to come out of the kennel. Patti had said Nikki was obedience, agility, and protection trained. I asked Patti if I could try and she said sure, so I gave Nikki a heel command and started walking away and she heeled and we started working. We got outside and she did everything I said. She did want to pull back to the house, but she

31

did everything I asked. Since Nikki was already trained, I did 50/50 of two different programs I offer—teaching the dog and teaching the owner, to get Patti to the point where she could walk Nikki in daylight."

The clients that don't come to Fred, he finds on his own, as in the case of the woman with two pit bulls. "I pulled into a gas station one day and saw a woman with two dogs in the back of her car," explains Fred. "One was an American Staffordshire, and the other was an English Staffordshire terrier, better known as 'pit bulls.' I gave her my card, and I didn't think too much about it. About a month later, I get a phone call in the wee hours, about five a.m. She was screaming and crying because the dogs were fighting, and she was all torn up trying to get them to stop. I made an appointment to see her and her husband at a restaurant. He's a real dominant figure, a bigwig in their small town. Men can get puffed up and they want to be macho. You ruin their ego when you tell them they're messing up their dog. He wasn't going to let me do anything unless I showed him how to do it.

"In situations like that, I usually say, 'You wouldn't have called me if your way was working.' Once he saw that I was for real and that I could do more with his dog than he could, he was intrigued. I worked their dogs and I kept telling the owners what the problem was: the dogs were fighting amongst themselves because they were picking up on the owners' chaos and aggression. The dogs were learning their behavior from the owners—they are highly sensitive to adrenaline aggression, and whatever is going on in the house—they understand it faster than people do. One dog was his and one was hers. So the owners had to work out what was going on between themselves in order to get their dogs to stop fighting."

With Porter, Fred was heavier on the American Standard method. "He's a big dog and he didn't have any confidence in Susan," he explains. "You have to meet him on his terms. He felt abandoned, he felt alone, and he wasn't socialized. You've got to realize his history. He's gonna have things that need to be addressed, and do things not just because of his breed, but because of the way he was raised."

After an initial consultation, Fred determined that he would work with Susan and Porter at their home but did not want to do so in the slippery conditions of winter. The approach of spring brought the opportunity for him to begin work.

One of the most important goals was to get Porter off of the thirty-foot chain he had been kept on, both literally and figuratively. Building Porter's enclosure was one practical step. Getting him the training he needed so that he could be taken out in public on a leash was the other practical step. Not only for his safety but also everyone else's.

And in order to do that, Fred first had to be sure that Susan could handle Porter. She says that in the beginning, she felt Fred's toughness, and wasn't always sure she was doing things the right way. But Fred explains, "We had to get her confidence up. You've got a hundred-pound woman, and here's this large, very intimidating animal that was wild and didn't know any better. I have to have her be serious and take charge. That's my responsibility. I have to get her to figure out what I do. I had to be serious and I had to be cautious. I had to figure her out, figure out her husband and her two kids, and figure out what I needed to do, how we're gonna get this done. Susan can trigger behavior because she's the closest to him. Once she showed him the confidence that she was going to proceed, he picked it up right away."

One exercise in particular addressed this very issue. Fred brought his German shepherd Rose to the house one day to do protection training. Fred asked Colin for a towel to wrap around his arm and told Susan to back herself completely against their garage door. Susan had no idea what Fred was about to do. "Keep your bottom pressed up against the garage," he told her. "Don't let it up, no matter what happens."

Fred gave Susan Rose's leash, then gave a verbal command to Rose in German, and that set her into protection mode. "Rose went into an aggressive state when she smelled my adrenaline," says Fred. "I flicked the towel at Susan. The towel was an extension of my hand. I left enough on the end of my hand so that when Rose went for me, she'd get the towel and not my hand."

Rose lunged at Fred in protection of Susan. Susan instinctively held back on the leash, as Fred had instructed her to before they began the exercise, causing Rose to spin in mid-air. "Rose went wild. She transformed completely from being calm and docile and went into protection mode. She lunged and I held on; she pulled so hard that she actually twisted in mid-air trying to get to Fred."

Fred adds that as soon as Rose landed, she came at him again until he told Susan to give a verbal command to "call Rose out" of protection mode. When Susan gave the command, Rose stopped immediately and Fred told Susan to put Rose in a heel position. "It was over as quickly as it started," says Fred. Susan's butt never left the garage wall and Fred taught her a valuable lesson in confidence.

Fred concludes, "Rose isn't violent. Porter isn't violent. I was teaching Susan that for every action that Porter has, she can have a reaction to stop him. His purpose, he says, was to "get Susan to understand that this could happen—Porter is not aggressive, but he can be defensive and go into aggression—but that she can control him."

There was another exercise that Fred did with Susan and Colin that proved to be particularly valuable to Susan. They were walking back down their driveway after working with Porter on a hike in the woods. Fred wanted to test Porter. As Colin walked with Porter in a heel in front of Susan and Fred, out of the blue Fred shoved Susan. Porter immediately sensed it and turned around and looked at Fred. They kept walking, and then Fred shoved Susan again. And again Porter turned, this time swinging his head fully around to look at Fred. They walked on, and when Fred shoved Susan a third time, Porter swung around, jumped up, and grabbed Fred's arm.

"Porter had Fred's arm in his mouth, but he did not bite down—he stopped Fred. He knew Fred was with us and accepted by us but he was clearly not happy with Fred's actions," Susan explains. "Fred then commented to me, 'If anyone decides to jump out of the woods at you, it'll be the last thing they do!' He described Porter as protective, not aggressive. In those days, I didn't know the difference. But now that lesson helps me to understand Porter, because just about everything with him is centered in his confidence and his protective nature."

Much more regular training routines included playground agility, along with other exercises to help stimulate Porter both mentally and physically, often using objects that are common in the nearby woods, such as logs, platforms, and balance beams for Porter to walk on, climb on, or jump over.

Once Fred had worked with Susan, he was able to get the rest of the family involved. He explains that though Porter will obey commands for both Colin and Susan, he'll do them differently for each of them, because his relationship is different with each of them.

After seven training sessions, it was time for Susan to take Porter out in public on the leash. "Did she ever tell you about the first time we took him downtown?" Fred asks me with a twinkle in his eye during one of our interviews. "She kept saying 'Well, what if a kid runs up to us?' and one did. Everything she was worried about encountering happened. But you know what? It was fine. Porter was fine. Because she was prepared." By "downtown" Fred refers to the heart of Loveland, where a buzz of activity, including residences, restaurants, and shops, marks the head of a popular bike trail.

This area tends to be a high-stress area for Porter, and Susan doesn't linger at the trailhead when she walks with him there. When she first started walking with him at the bike trail, every loud noise, such as a passing fire truck, startled Porter. If too many people crowd around, he gets anxious and backs away, nearer to Susan, and he especially doesn't like to be circled, with anyone behind him. Bicycles in general also frighten Porter; he's used to cyclists passing him and Susan as they walk, but he won't greet someone seated on a bike who has stopped to inquire.

Susan does have protocols she follows when other dogs are near, and when people are interested in meeting Porter, which happens increasingly as locals recognize him. But Fred doesn't place limitations on Porter in terms of how he interacts with people. "Here's Porter all in a nutshell. He's going to approach you," he says, speaking of how Porter decides if he wants to greet people. Porter will approach the person if they are standing still. If they move, he will usually abort the encounter, the only exception being the handful of people that Porter considers part of his pack. "He's really independent in his thinking. Some people can approach him. He's a great judge of character."

But he really credits Susan with Porter's progress. "We all had a piece of the puzzle, but she's the one who put the pieces together to make the story what it is today. She's done it, she's put the time and the work in. I just gave her the tools. That's how she's accomplished what she's done."

Wolf by Nature

Lois Crisler says of the wolfdog in her book *Arctic Wild*, "The wolfdog is … liable to be more dangerous than either parent … If the combination occurred of a dog's fierce heart and a wolf's indifference toward man, the animal could be ruthless … but the opposite is possible too: a wolf's solicitude and intensity, plus a dog's human orientation. Then you get an animal that has greatness." There is a greatness about Porter that people can sense even from afar, or as they approach Susan for the chance to meet him.

They are also drawn to Porter's magnificent beauty and presence. They will comment on his size (about 120 pounds at his full winter weight), or his thick fur (also at its most impressive when he has his full winter coat). In one instance when I was walking with Susan and Porter, four girls on bicycles were riding on the trail, and passed cordially to our left. They were speaking a foreign language, and as the lead rider passed us, she looked over her shoulder, smiled, and made a comment to her friends. The only words in English were the last three: "*Game of Thrones!*"

Many ask if he's friendly and if they may pet him. While these are normal inquiries for a dog, the answers are more complex for a wolfdog, and reflect the fact that he is, according to his DNA, part wolf.

What this means in Porter's case, especially since he was mistreated by his first owner, is that there is a protocol for meeting and interacting with him.

Wolves are typically more skittish than aggressive around people, and "generally...don't attack man," as Edward Hoagland notes in his essay "Red Wolves and Black Bears."

Porter, perhaps more so than other dogs, must be introduced to people by having them stand still with their arms at their sides. Porter then might approach and sniff. If he does so and is comfortable, Susan will often hand the person a treat to give him. If he backs away, or doesn't want to approach, Susan respects that.

When it comes to other dogs, Porter is not amenable to them, and Susan's protocol is to pull him to the side of the trail, put him in a sit, and hold her leash close to the collar when someone with another dog passes. Porter's responses to passing dogs may vary from barely taking any notice to attempting to pop up in aggression, which is why this protocol is in place. Fred explains that subtle communication takes place between dogs that humans can't see or understand. This could include a challenge issued from another dog to Porter, which in turn compels him to respond the way he does.

There are, of course, exceptions to these rules of behavior. On rare occasions, Porter will fully accept someone almost right away, or after a very short period of time. Over time Porter has also accepted Colin and Susan's other dogs, and there are two others that Porter has accepted as well: he can be in close proximity with their neighbor Gwen's dog Maggie, and he and Bob, the golden retriever who belonged to their neighbor Todd, became buddies. Susan has also begun to socialize him with other wolfdogs in a group of wolfdog owners who hike with their animals once a week.

The following events are examples of lessons learned for both Susan and Porter, lessons in overcoming fear and in learning trust for both of them. They also serve as guideposts on Porter's path of growth from a mistreated, unsocialized animal to a wolfdog who expresses his innate intelligence and ability to enjoy the freedom of living off the chain that is safe and harmonious for him, for Susan, and for everyone with whom he comes into contact.

White Dog

What Susan refers to as the "white dog" incident happened early on, before she started working with Fred. It remains one of the most vivid in her memory and even prompted her to consider re-homing Porter.

One winter Saturday afternoon, Susan was walking Porter in a nearby neighborhood. As she passed one house, she noticed a woman standing in her yard talking on her cell phone. The woman's two unleashed Chihuahuas reacted loudly and aggressively as Susan and Porter approached. Susan almost didn't proceed, for fear that the dogs would leave their yard. "But then I thought that surely they had an electric fence," she explains. "I needed to overcome my fear, and we had a right to be there." As they passed on the other side of the road, both dogs ran into the street. One charged them, crossing the street and snapping and lunging at Porter.

Susan describes her efforts to contain the situation and keep Porter from reacting: "I kept calling out to the lady to call off her dog, all the while spinning with Porter on his leash to try to keep him from the other dog's face." But the dog had come in so close to them, to Susan's legs, that she couldn't prevent Porter from finally reacting. "I looked down and he had the white dog in his mouth. At that point the woman finally saw what was happening and got off of her cell phone. She ran down from her yard yelling for her husband to help." Susan commanded Porter to drop the dog a couple of times, and he eventually did. The white dog lay there motionless and bloodied.

It's always easy in a situation like this to cast blame in one direction or the other, and Susan was mortified. "I felt awful." But the woman expressed to Susan that her dog shouldn't have left the yard—that she should have been paying better attention and should have had better control over her pets.

Susan gave the woman her phone number and she called Susan the next day and took full responsibility for the incident, saying that her dog had done that before. She never asked Susan to pay the vet bill, and the Chihuahua recovered, but the incident vexed Susan for months. "Walking home that day, I just thought 'I can't do this. I can't keep an animal that does these things.'"

Fred later explained to Susan that Porter was just handling what he perceived to be an annoyance—a threat to his space and to Susan. "He was not being offensive, but defensive," he says, and that Porter made an intelligent choice to stop the annoyance, but not kill the dog. "If he had been offensive, he would have crushed that dog."

Pit Bulls

It could be argued that the biggest things pit bulls have in common with wolfdogs is that they are misunderstood and that unfortunate incidents are often caused by mishandling or lack of training on the owners' parts. Two incidents involving pit bulls have tested the calm preparedness that Susan gained in her training sessions with Fred.

One hot summer day along the river, Susan sent her daughter Jelena, who was walking with her and Porter, to jog ahead to see if there were any people with unleashed dogs nearby. When Jelena returned with a "coast's clear," Susan took Porter down to the water for a much-needed dip. As they stepped to the water's edge, a loose pit bull rushed up behind them from out of nowhere. The owner yelled from a distance that his dog, a female, was friendly. In spite of the leash law, the pit bull had no collar and no leash. Nor was she obedient or responsive to her owner's commands. "People always think they are the exception to the laws that are in place for everyone's safety and protection," says Susan. "I yelled 'get your dog!' as Porter swung around to protect himself. The pit bull kept lunging, and so did all 120 pounds of Porter. I was stuck—I couldn't back up or I would be in the river. If I fell down and became vulnerable, Porter would escalate and likely kill in defense of me."

The confrontation continued: the pit bull was relentless in approaching, the owner didn't want to get near enough to help separate them, and Porter clearly wanted to fight. Jelena fled the river screaming in fear. Susan says the owner did not move to get his dog. Instead he continually yelled for Susan to get control of Porter, though his dog was the one loose, while she had Porter on a short leash. Susan was backed up to the river and trying to control an agitated Porter, with the pit bull blocking any exit strategy. All the while, onlookers gawked, and kayakers on the river backpaddled as the scene unfolded.

It came to a head when the pit bull lunged once more, and Porter flipped it. "I thought I was going to see him gut it," recalls Susan. "But I realized I needed to do as Fred taught me. So I jerked Porter's prong collar once more and actually stepped back into the river. I kept solid footing and yelled for the guy to come get his dog."

The owner of the pit bull finally did that, but yelled at Susan in the process, "That ain't no dog. That's a wolf."

One of the kayakers called out and offered help after he identified himself as a vet. Shaken, Susan climbed out of the riverbed, and the first person she saw was a trainer who had previously encountered Susan and Porter on the bike trail and expressed an interest in working with them. "He appeared like an angel," says Susan. "I felt horrible about the situation, and after walking with me and talking with me to help calm me down, he told me that I did everything as I should have. In the end, he reminded me that neither dog had gotten hurt."

Ironically, the trainer had his own pit bull with him that day, and asked Susan to walk behind them so that Porter could smell them and get used to his dog. After a short time they were able to walk side by side, and eventually they stopped to talk again four feet apart, and both dogs lay down at their feet. "Seeing this trainer right after that horrible incident was clearly a needed blessing," says Susan.

While pit bulls seem to be a popular local pet, and Susan has encountered several on the trail without any trouble, there was one other incident, once again with an unleashed pit bull, that stands out in Susan's memory. She recalls a group of about three or four teenagers sitting on a bench with a pit bull at their feet. Though she thought she spotted a leash, Susan instinctively stepped off the trail to put more space between them. It was the right call, because the dog was loose, and immediately charged her and Porter, again severely frightening Jelena. "I yelled at them to get their dog, but no one moved to do anything. They just looked on."

The pit bull turned to attack again, and Porter was now fully agitated. Finally one of the kids in the group came over to get their dog. Susan turned the incident into a teaching moment. "I was flustered, but it was an opportunity to remind them about the importance of controlling their dog and obeying the leash laws. I was angry because it's my job to protect Porter from harming another dog, even in self-defense—because he's a wolfdog, he won't get a second chance."

Fred reiterates that in all of the incidents involving other dogs, "Porter's never been the aggressor, always the defender."

Furry Friends

In spite of these challenges, Porter has also had positive interactions and relationships with other dogs, including the other family pets. Colin and Susan's two other dogs, Sweetie and Scout (both females, both medium-sized and mixed-breed), were already well-established in the family and had their own enclosure when Porter arrived on the scene. "We first let him loose in their pen, but with his leash on, the same day we got him. It felt uncomfortable very quickly though. He got rough and made noises that sounded intimidating. We quickly grabbed the leash and removed him from their pen. Before we built his enclosure, he was chained to a tree right next to their fenced yard, so he got used to them."

Porter does make noises when he first greets the girl dogs or after his walks, that Susan recognizes as "talk." It's a low, guttural noise that can sound threatening, but Susan explains that it means he is happy to see them. "I remember sitting with Porter, when he was new to us and still on the chain and waiting for his enclosure to be built. I would pet him and talk to him, but as soon as I would hear those noises, I would get up and leave because it made me uncomfortable. We laugh now because he sounds like Chewbacca from *Star Wars*. But when we didn't know him, those were scary sounds. After a year or so, Porter began talking more and more to his sisters. He does this as we walk together now, usually standing in front of the person walking them so the girls know without a doubt that they are part of his pack!"

Sometimes he is a little too fresh with Scout, though, and she's not afraid to let him know. "After months and then years of walking him with the girls, we realized that little Scout won't take his crap—he is just an annoying big brother to her."

Colin and Susan's cat, Lucky, made good on his name by fearlessly befriending Porter, although Colin and Susan worried about him when Porter arrived. Lucky had a habit of running down the driveway chasing alongside Susan's car as she came home, or running up to her with his tail in the air. In one instance, he came running toward her as she walked Porter down the driveway. Lucky came right up to them, jumped up, and head-butted Porter on the nose. But Lucky had also spent months prior to this patiently getting to know Porter. He was an adventurous indoor/outdoor cat, who wandered the woods and neighborhood and always returned home at night. But with Porter on a chain, that presented a concern. But Lucky's intelligence and patience put those concerns to rest. He would spend hours laying down near Porter, but just outside of his thirty-foot radius. Once the enclosure was built, Lucky moved even closer to Porter, until one day he was spotted rubbing Porter's fence and Porter reciprocated by bumping the fence on his side! Clearly he wasn't afraid to make friends!

Baby Love

It's not surprising that Porter has always demonstrated more of a trust and affinity for the kids who want to meet him than for the adults. But as in all things, Susan prefers to control the situation, and of course to employ caution in doing so. Even in the rare situations where she hasn't been in control, Porter has shown himself to be a gentleman.

49

One day when Susan had been running with Porter on his leash alongside her, his close heel caused their legs to become entangled as they turned at the bottom of a cul-de-sac on a side street near Susan's residence. "I tripped and fell flat, and lost my hold on Porter's leash," she says. "Porter was trotting away from me up the street toward another, busier road with traffic, and beyond that, an alpaca farm."

She got up and ran after him. He looked back but kept moving away from her. Coming toward them was a tall nanny, all in black, accompanying a mother pushing a baby stroller. The nanny jumped between Porter and the baby carriage and formed a huge X with her body. This caused Porter to stop for a moment, giving Susan just enough time to catch up and grab his leash. "My heart was racing a tad on that one!" she admits.

But that wasn't the only incident involving a child. "Set your small child down in front of a strange wolfdog (or any strange dog for that matter)" said no one ever. Yet that's exactly what one woman did. A mother holding a toddler approached Susan and Porter in the parking lot near the bike trail, and asked, "Can we pet your dog?"

Before Susan could answer and explain to the woman how people need to be introduced to Porter, she plopped her fourteen-month-old down in front of him. "I was horrified," says

Susan. The toddler stood unsteadily, and he was as tall as Porter's head. Before Susan could react, Porter stretched his neck forward and gently touched the child's face with his nose. According to Susan, the child squealed, and a startled Porter jumped back and hid behind Susan's legs.

"I mean, if I were to say to a mother, will you put your child in front of my wolfdog so I can see what he will do," says Susan, "would she agree? I hope not. But now I know."

Food Issues

In one of her conversations with Porter's former owner, Susan remembers him telling her that after he and his family moved out of their house, he was only able to get back over there every few days to feed Porter—meaning that Porter often had to survive on whatever wandered into the thirty-foot radius of his chain. This undoubtedly created a protectiveness of his food, and Colin and Susan have occasionally witnessed this side of him.

Porter can dart after an interesting scent in the bushes in an instant. In all the times that he investigated something, Susan never expected him to come out with a rabbit in his mouth. And when he did, Susan describes a soft little gray foot was all that stuck out of it. While it was horrifying in the moment, she eventually found a sense of humor about it. "Before I could say 'No, drop!' there was one big crunch, two little crunches, and then he sucked it down like spaghetti!"

While Porter's enclosure was being built, Susan and Colin had no choice but to keep him on the chain he came with. And even though he was well-fed and cared for, his habit of catching whatever came close enough was hard to leave behind. One night a raccoon wandered up. Unlike Susan and Colin's other two dogs, who were barking loudly in alert, Porter, by nature (and out of necessity, in the past), remained completely silent. But the barking of the other two dogs brought Susan and Colin to their bedroom window in time to witness Porter taking out the raccoon. "He watched the raccoon as it wandered unknowingly into his radius. Then he pounced and shook, and it was over," recalls Susan.

Colin didn't think it was wise to go down there in the dark to try to take the carcass from Porter and planned to remove it the next morning. But the next morning it was nowhere in sight. "We actually wondered if he had eaten it all overnight. Or, more optimistically, we hoped it hadn't been killed but had wandered out of Porter's area." But a few days later Porter had the raccoon in his mouth again and was dragging it around.

"So we watched him. It was remarkable. He dug a very

52

deep hole. Jammed the raccoon in it. Used his nose as a shovel to cover it and then used his nose as a hammer. The burial of the raccoon was so perfect that had we not seen where he put it, we wouldn't have known where it was." Once they knew where it was buried, Colin was able to dig it up and dispose of it while Susan walked Porter later that day.

While Colin and Susan can feed Porter from inside his enclosure, his food and water stand is built so that the young man who usually cares for Porter when they are away can feed him from outside the enclosure. Wisdom dictates this measure, based on Porter's protectiveness and sometimes even possessiveness of his food and treats.

When Susan has given him a raw beef bone as a treat (which he no longer gets due to the changes in his diet), she has left the enclosure immediately, and doesn't go back in until he has buried it or left it alone for a while. When he does so, she knows that its value has lessened enough for her to safely re-enter his enclosure.

But this was a lesson hard learned when she gave him a pumpkin one afternoon and returned to his enclosure to check on him later that night, as is her habit. She had given him a smaller pumpkin the week before and he'd devoured it. But this one was larger, and he had hardly touched it when she entered the pen that night. Instead, it remained in front of his doghouse within the enclosure. It was pitch dark. She had entered the pen as usual to say goodnight, and was talking quietly to Porter, who lay in his doghouse. He must have remembered his pumpkin, because he pulled back, disappearing into the doghouse. He came out lunging, snapping, and growling. He stood protectively over the pumpkin; his hackles were up and his eyes were hard. Susan was in trouble—she was now stuck on the wrong side of the pumpkin. Porter and the pumpkin were now separating her from the gate. Susan's heart raced as she stood face to face with a highly agitated animal that looked nothing like her much-loved Porter.

Susan eventually decided to circumnavigate the pen to reach the gate by going the long way around. As she came up past the tire he likes to lie in near the fence, he lunged at her and bared his teeth.

"It took me almost an hour to get out of his pen that night," she says. "His teeth were clacking, and his hackles were up. That's when I spoke out loud to him, saying, 'But I love you, Porter,' which distracted him for a split second—he turned away from me and back toward the pumpkin, which gave me time to make the three steps to the gate and get out." Though it was late at night, she texted Fred, who assured her that Porter had reacted that way because of the way he was handled and treated by his former owner, forcing him to protect everything that was edible for his own survival, and that it was unlikely that Porter would have actually hurt Susan. She wasn't entirely sure about that, but took comfort in his words nonetheless. Now she doesn't give him anything that he can't consume in a short period of time.

Only one other time prior to that incident has Susan felt at risk in Porter's enclosure, and she accepts blame for not being as observant as she should have of Porter's body language and not being attuned to how tense he was as she entered.

She describes how he was pacing and clearly agitated—by what, exactly, she doesn't know. "I had gone in at dusk, and I sat on his platform. He wouldn't settle down or hop up to sit with me like he usually does. Then it dawned on me that Porter was 'off' and that this was not a good environment for me. Porter had been pacing in circles and when I jumped down, he turned his agitation toward me, and I moved as fast as I could toward the gate."

Within seconds, she was out with the gate closed, but Porter charged the fence, snapping and lunging, with eyes hardened. Colin arrived at that point, having realized that something wasn't right, and kicked the fence as Porter charged it. "It was late at night, and I heard a commotion," Colin explains.

He went on to say that Porter was acting in a way he hadn't seen since an incident in a cabin when he and Susan first adopted him, which he describes at length in a later chapter. "I was frustrated."

Two possible causes seem the most likely. The first is winter wolf syndrome, wherein a seasonal hormonal behavior change can occur in high-content wolfdogs, according to the Southern Ohio Wolf Sanctuary's website. A second possibility again points back to his life on the chain with his former owner. "We don't know how many times he had to defend himself against coyotes—we don't know that he wasn't attacked when he was on the chain," Fred points out. "When coyotes run in packs, they're hunting and it's scary, it's really eerie. He would go into defensive mode of his area. Colin broke the cycle of defensive mode by kicking the fence." Susan confirms that there were coyotes in the woods nearby that night when she entered Porter's enclosure. "I had even heard them howling prior to going to see Porter. I remember thinking how lovely, and yet it was also chilling."

Colin concludes, "We're always cognizant of the fact that he's part wolf, and we take nothing for granted. We watch him carefully to see if he's behaving abnormally, especially after we're inside the enclosure."

PORTER

37.5% Wolf
25% German Shepherd Dog
12.5% Siberian Husky
25% Breed Group(s)

PARENTS

Wolf
Breed Group(s)
German Shepherd Dog

Wolf
Siberian Husky
German Shepherd Dog
Breed Group(s)

GRANDPARENTS

Wolf

Breed Group(s)
German Shepherd Dog

Wolf
Siberian Husky

German Shepherd Dog
Breed Group(s)

GREAT GRANDPARENTS

Wolf   Wolf   Breed   German   Wolf   Siberian   German   Breed
                Group(s) Shepherd   Husky   Shepherd   Group(s)
                         Dog   Dog

PORTER'S BREED BY PERCENTAGE *

* Porter has been DNA tested through both Embark and Wisdom Panel. Both tests showed the exact same percentage for his main breed (wolf). But a Wisdom Panel veterinarian gave a more detailed explanation of his DNA, above what their standard kit showed. This explanation showed that his main breed is Western Gray Wolf and that there is an additional percentage that also shows Eastern Gray Wolf as well as Eastern Coyote (which could be a misread and actually means more wolf). The vet's report went on to say that although Wisdom Panel does not include the different subtypes of Wolf within the standard pet report, for the US products, they do have the genetic signatures for the two subtypes of Gray Wolf (Eastern and Western). The subtypes were not included in Porter's actual report, but the subtype information is present in the data to which the veterinary science team had access and which was shared in the separate report given to Susan. See pie chart below for details.

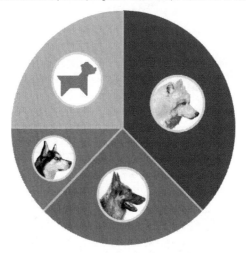

● 37.5% Western Gray Wolf

● 25% German Shepherd Dog

● 12.5% Siberian Husky

● 25% Breed Group(s)

- Asian
- Wild Canids*
- Herding

* (additional percentage of wild canid includes Eastern Gray Wolf and Eastern Coyote, which may just be a false read for even more Eastern Gray Wolf)

Recreated by Beezley Design Studio based on the original by Wisdom Panel

Baby Porter!

A hard memory...
six years on a chain.

First walk with Susan.
Will she adopt him?

Safe now, but a lot of work to do. First step, off the chain! Enclosure coming soon! (Photo by Susan's son JC)

Happy & Loved

Walk on a summer's day.

Look at that smile!

Safe and happy in his enclosure.

Curled up in the hay.

63

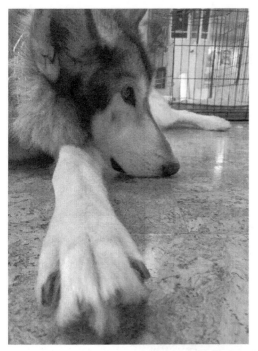

Chillin' in the A/C.

Thirsty boy!
Photo by
Mary C.
Johnson

Furry Friends

Porter and Lucky cat.

Porter with Jelena,
Sweetie (l) and Scout (r)

The siblings he
never knew
(l to r):
Sayan, Jake,
Willard and
Joanie.

66

While we don't have any photos of Susan's neighbor
Todd, he is an important part of Porter's story. And
though Porter and Todd's golden retriever Bob didn't
always get along, they eventually became buddies.

Mike and Jim of Mike's
Mobile Vet Service saying
hello.

Jim and Porter.

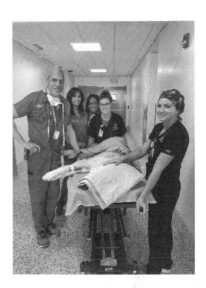

Porter's team at Ohio State
University Veterinary
Medical Center

69

Fred with Porter above, and with his pack below, (l to r): Rocko, Sky and Rose.

Hanging with Gwen in her driveway

Now that we're on the porch together. . .

Treats first, kisses later!

72

Gwen's friend Debbie getting
comfort from Porter.

73

Porter and his buddy Roger

Porter with Jason the Ranger

Susan and Dale outside of Porter's
enclosure

Colin with Porter and the kids on a fateful camping trip
(above), and walking together (below).

Porter and JC lounging together (above), and
impromptu sweetness (below)

Jelena with Susan and Porter

Susan walking with her
boy.
Above right photo by
Mary C. Johnson

Susan getting love from her boy.

Me (aka Porter's "Cali/California Mama"
with Susan and our boy.

A walk in the woods.
Colin and Susan are nearby, but I got to
hold the leash for the photo.

83

Love nips!

Getting a birthday kiss.
No better way to celebrate!

Andrew and me with winter Wolfie.

Andrew getting nuzzles after his first walk with Porter and the family.

Car buddies!

A New Pack

Since Susan is taking Porter on regular walks with Ohio River Wolves, he is learning to socialize with other wolfdogs and their owners.

Cozying up to Arya.

Getting used to
Rama and Raoul.
The boys are back in town!

On the lookout with the lovely Tiamat in the distance.
Porter definitely prefers the company
of the ladies in the pack!

Porter is gradually growing to trust ORW member Brian, walking here with Kaden.

Porter's People

"Porter sees something he needs in those he accepts, or something he has to give to them." – Fred Russell

"Porter chose these individuals carefully and loves them fiercely." – Colin

Colin

     I knew Susan's husband Colin first in childhood, when our families attended the same church. He and I later attended the same college, and then the same church in our adult years, where I also got to know Susan. Even as a teenager, I remember Colin as being solid in character and stature, trustworthy, principled, and kind. He is a strong support in his co-ownership of Porter with Susan.

     When I ask Colin to describe his relationship with Porter, he says, "It immediately makes me think of how I've grown and changed since we've had Porter." He goes on to describe it as an "opportunity for the outpouring of love toward another being."

     That opportunity began almost immediately, and, as many do, required much of both Colin and Porter, each needing to learn the trust on which to build that love.

The family had already scheduled a winter camping trip in a cabin for Christmas before Susan and Colin adopted Porter. Not fully understanding the extent of Porter's socialization (or lack thereof) and thinking he would be much like their other dogs and the wolfdog they'd had before, Colin and Susan packed up their gear and Porter, and headed for the cabin they'd rented. Porter had only ridden in a car twice in his life, so they tranquilized him to make the four-hour journey easier. But even with sedation, he chewed through two seatbelts before they had driven two miles.

Once there, they realized that they couldn't leave Porter outside on the chain, because people had unleashed dogs in the park. They didn't want a person or another animal to walk into his area and have a problem. They were forced to bring him inside.

As they began to settle in, Colin noticed that the leash had become entangled around one of Porter's hind legs. When Colin attempted to lift Porter's leg to untangle the leash, Porter turned around and bit Colin's hand. In reaction, Colin struck back. Porter was backed up to a kitchen wall. Fear filled the cabin as a full-grown man faced off with a 120-pound wolfdog, Colin in a defensive stance, prepared to do whatever he had to in order to protect his family, and Porter growling, teeth bared, doing what he thought he had to in order to protect himself. It was a truly frightening moment, one that sent their two children running from the room screaming and in tears.

Susan says she doesn't know what prompted her to do what she did then. She stepped between Colin and Porter and said to the animal, "It's all right, Porter. It's all right." It broke the tension and allowed them to regain control of the situation.

There are many ways to interpret that moment. One might be to label it foolish for a small woman to step in front of a frightened animal that clearly outweighed her. What is clear is that something other than brute force was needed in that moment, and Susan provided that.

When Colin reflects back on that night, he explains his approach. "Back then I was probably a little more bullheaded, more 'let's do it,' and if it's gonna get done, it's got to be my way...and this is my idea. With Porter, I saw a situation that needed correcting, not realizing that there was a different or better way to handle the situation, so that's really a lesson for life."

It was a long night in the cabin, not restful for anyone, and with the realization that Porter was not an animal to accompany the family on a camping trip, they cancelled the rest of their weekend, and hiked ten miles to wear Porter out before making the journey home. That night in the cabin marked a rough beginning for Porter and his new family, a journey not without doubts and fear on both sides at times, but neither without its rewards. "We were willing to go out on a limb for him, but he's given us so much more back as a result."

Colin thoughtfully recalls a book he read thirty years ago titled *Kinship with All Life* by J. Allen Boone. "The basic theme of books like that is that there's so much to learn from our relationship to all animals. There's a lot we can learn from nature if we're willing to listen for that experience, so that's something that Porter's helping drive home right here in our home, in our present experience." Colin adds that he's encouraged to reread those books, which have an even more profound meaning for him now.

Colin describes Porter as "intelligent, dedicated to his pack, joyful, insightful…he expresses love as he looks up at somebody who walks with him, and people who interact with him in turn express that in their own lives. I think he chooses people to be in his pack for a reason and he chooses not to allow people in his pack for reasons…that are good ones for him."

When speaking to others about Porter, the first thing Colin does is establish that Porter is a rescue. "We didn't have him bred; we didn't buy him because we wanted a wolfdog. He was left and was going to be put down and the vet reached out to us," he explains, quickly adding words of caution. "Doing this is not for everybody. I encourage anyone who wants a pet—any pet—to think about the time they're willing to spend with that pet and if that would be sufficient for that pet's healthy being." He describes the commitment to caring for an animal, especially one like Porter, as akin to a marriage; there has to be a mutual benefit, with the human giving something to the animal.

"I tell people how the experience has changed us—the effect it's had on the family." He details working with a professional trainer, meeting wonderful neighbors, and going on long walks with Susan and their other two dogs. "It's great when he bumps us [a wolfdog "hug" in which Porter leans in and rubs across your legs, scenting you and showing affection] and looks up and makes a real connection with us. And we're able to practice the skills that Fred taught us. You hear people talk about something like this in terms of how much we're doing. But I'm getting so much more out of the engagement than I've put in. That's how I see our relationship with Porter."

Jelena

The younger of Colin and Susan's two children, Jelena is curious, kindhearted, loving, and soft-natured. During my visits to the house, I learned that she loves to sing and play the piano. She has learned some Elton John tunes that we both love to sing along with as she plays. Jelena is also devoted to her part-time work and school programs as she prepares to attend college when she is ready. Porter seems to have assumed a role of affection and protection with her.

Like the other family members, Jelena says that in the beginning it wasn't easy to get used to him. "I felt unsure, and I wondered how it would be to care for him, and whether or not it would be too much for us."

She now considers him to be a "beautiful animal" and clarifies that she means that in terms of both appearance and disposition. Jelena describes getting bumps from Porter, and that one of her favorite ways to return his affection is to give him "surprise love" when she and Susan are walking with him. This is where they stop, call Porter close to them, and pet him and speak to him affectionately, usually as he's leaning into their legs.

"He's an interesting animal with interesting ways of communicating with people," she concludes.

JC is older brother to Jelena, and upon first meeting him, his warmth and engaging smile reminded me that if I'd had a brother, I would have wanted him to be like JC. He looks out for Jelena, and even as a busy college student, his connection to home and family remains strong. JC has held an interesting position within Porter's pack, with full acceptance, but not without the need for caution.

At one point JC took a high school friend into Porter's enclosure, along with Susan. After a few minutes, Porter became uncomfortable and growled at JC. Fred surmised that Porter may see JC as somewhat of a rival, at least within the space of his enclosure. Since then, JC does not go inside the enclosure at all, but remains part of Porter's pack, and continues to be part of his care whenever he's home from college.

Oddly enough, JC has no recollection of the incident. "I don't think I have forgotten because I'm traumatized in any way. It wasn't surprising, as incidents such as these have occurred in the past, but I definitely don't hold it against him. He's a wild animal, and I don't think there's ever a point where we'll be able to say, 'we did it, he's domesticated.' It's kind of similar with people, they have their flaws and habits, and while they can work to grow out of them, these tendencies still can surface. In Porter's case, we just have to be mindful of them without letting them define his existence. Still have all the love for that boy."

Outside of Porter's enclosure, they are best buddies. "It's been kind of cool, because I've learned to observe his behaviors and not over-read them—there's an understanding between us. It's just very natural," he continues. "I never feel like I have to force it in any way. You can kind of just pick up on his energy. He's just like a goofy guy that bumps into you and is happy to see you. It's been a lot about acceptance—accepting him for what he is, for the wolf self that he is."

JC also sees what adopting Porter has meant to the family as a whole. "What I've loved most is seeing how he's brought our family closer together," he concludes. "I think of all that we've learned about how to best care for him, and about what he needs."

Todd

I never had the opportunity to meet Todd, but feel as if I know him from all that Susan has shared about him. The evidence of his influence on Susan, on Porter, and on their situation is strong in the affection with which she speaks of him.

If any of Susan's neighbors in close proximity had objected to Susan having Porter, out of fear that he would get loose and harm them or their pets, she would have had to re-home him. And if any of them would have had a reason for concern, it would have been Todd and his wife. But "Todd is the reason we kept Porter," says Susan emphatically. "He was Porter's first friend and advocate even though Porter literally wanted to kill Todd's golden retriever, Bob. Initially I was so fearful, but Todd took a serious interest in helping me with Porter."

She goes on to explain that Todd would wait for her to get home from work and wave her down in the driveway. "Go get the big boy and bring him over," he'd say. It was Todd who gave Porter his one and only bath. Porter doesn't allow any grooming. But like a full-blooded wolf, he grooms himself immaculately.

Todd also drove to a nearby park in search of Susan to be sure a loose German shepherd hadn't bothered her and Porter. Susan says that Todd would always be out with an umbrella if she was caught in the rain while walking Porter, and that he also gifted her a high-powered flashlight for night walks and an insulated men's winter work suit to be sure that she stayed warm in cold-weather walks with Porter.

He often sat in Porter's enclosure while Susan was at work and talked to him. "That made me a little nervous, to say the least, but at the time, Todd and I were like a team." Todd also braved taking Porter for a walk once when the family was on vacation. "I didn't know he would do that, either, but he loved Porter and was trying to provide for him." And in one instance when another neighbor's German shepherds accosted Susan and Porter, circling them, Todd came out right away to offer comfort. "I couldn't have gotten through those first years with Porter if it weren't for Todd and the mental support he lent me and the friendship he showed to both me and Porter," says Susan.

Eventually, not only did Porter accept Todd's golden retriever Bob, but they actually became friends. Sadly, in August of 2015, Todd passed away suddenly while working at his computer. Though he'd lost Bob by that time, his puppy, Clyde, was by his side.

Todd's wife, also named Susan, reflects back on his clear affection for Porter, and for Susan as well. "He believed that Porter was a special dog and that Susan was a special person. He reminded Todd of our first dog, a 125-pound husky-Malamute mix. More times than Susan probably knew about, he would go and sit with Porter." She also says they considered taking Porter themselves, when they thought Susan and Colin might re-home him after some of the challenges, but that Todd felt he owed it to Bob not to bring in another dog or show favoritism. "He could also see that Porter needed someone like Susan to help him overcome the treatment he received from his former owner," she says. "I understand Todd's instant bond with Porter, and his desire for him to have a good life."

A cherished stuffed-animal tiger from Todd is the only such toy to have survived Porter's chewing. It remains inside his indoor kennel to this day.

Gwen

Susan's neighbor Gwen is one of Porter's people that I most wanted to meet. But I also wanted to measure up, so to speak. Gwen has a matriarchal presence that is kind and comforting, but also no-nonsense. She isn't shy about pointing out Susan's tardiness, for instance, and on one of my visits, when the temperature had dropped, she looked me and said, smiling, "You need to leave your little dresses at home, Miss L.A.!" I had fit right in.

But Gwen is also generous of spirit. She often makes dinner for Susan to pick up on her way home from work for the family. She's showered me and my husband with gifts, as well as Susan and Colin, and other neighbors she loves. Gwen has definitely become far more than just a neighbor—her friendship with Colin and Susan has expanded to include a couple of road trips with them. They lived only a short distance from each other but never knew it until recent years. "I first saw Susan walking Porter in the evenings and had to find out about him," Gwen recalls.

Susan remembers that Gwen finally ventured down her driveway to the road on one such evening and exclaimed, "I have to meet this big beautiful boy!"

"I was anxious to find out if he was a full-blooded wolf, as he certainly looked like he was," Gwen says. "He had his full coat then and was gorgeous."

He did let her approach that day, but he also takes his time warming up to people, even those he chooses to have in his pack. Susan gave Gwen a treat to give him, and "that's when the love affair started," says Gwen.

Over time, though, Gwen's relationship with Porter solidified into acceptance. It took several times of Susan stopping to visit Gwen on her walks with Porter before he fully accepted her. Gwen's yellow lab, Maggie, who is often outside with Gwen, doesn't get close to Porter, being constrained by Gwen's electric fence. "He was eager to take the treats I offered him without hesitation," she says. "He does get a little vocal if Maggie gets her treats before him."

She follows Susan's protocol of setting a treat down in

front of him and asking him to wait before giving the verbal "okay." She throws Maggie's treats to catch, but Porter doesn't have the same jumping skills. "I finally figured out that he needed them more at his eye level and I started throwing them closer to that; then he started catching them. Now he's pretty good and catches them about seventy-five to eighty percent of the time."

The two dogs are fine being across from each other in the driveway, with Maggie staying within her electric fence and Susan keeping Porter close on his lead. While Maggie is not afraid of him, and Porter is comfortable on her front porch and in her driveway or yard, Gwen fears that jealousy might provoke one of them to misbehave, so caution wins the day.

When Gwen did gain Porter's full acceptance, it was without reservation. "I was not prepared for the first hug I received—he almost knocked me down!—but I felt like he had accepted me and was ready to be my friend. He feels like a special friend, not just a wolfdog to me. I do get a kiss on the cheek if I ask him to kiss me," she says.

Gwen certainly does spoil him, not just with dog treats but also, beef bones that she gets directly from her butcher, until recently when Porter's diet changed. "I knew those bones were meaty and more like the ones in the wild."

She has also witnessed firsthand how, once Porter decides to connect with someone, it is significant and unequivocal. Susan brought Porter to visit Gwen's cousin Debbie, who had been battling cancer and loved wolves. Debbie had even visited a wolf sanctuary when she was able. She sat on her porch when Susan arrived with Porter and he went right to her and gave her a wolfdog kiss on her cheek.

"It was like he knew she needed that," says Gwen. "He seems to sense when a person is good."

Debbie passed away not long after that, and the picture capturing her moment with Porter graced her service at the funeral parlor.

Roger

Roger is a kind, reserved man with a warm smile, but he's also one of few words. He's not a social man, and we've laughed at the realization that this could be one reason why Porter has taken to him—two lone wolves, comfortable with the pack they've chosen, and needing no other. Since Roger isn't an easy person to reach, my first meeting with him was only by chance, when he happened to be on the bike trail walking at the same time that Susan and I were walking Porter.

Since then, Susan and Gwen and I have enjoyed a couple

of meals with Roger, and gotten to know him a little better. A widower, Roger lives alone and mostly keeps to himself, so he was surprised to have been included in a special evening at Susan's home that involved a reading of an excerpt of this book, along with another performance reading, and a cookout with family and others in Porter's people pack. It was that night when I felt that perhaps Roger sensed how special he had become, not only to Porter, but to others as well.

Roger says that he saw Susan and Porter on the bike trail a few times before he decided to approach them. "He's an amazing animal," Roger offers quietly with a soft smile. "Susan's done a wonderful job with him."

"Porter liked Roger right away. We had passed him several times and one day Roger finally stopped and asked, 'Is that a wolf?' and we chatted, and Porter was very calm with him." After the next two or three times they encountered Roger on the trail, Porter allowed Roger to pet him. Soon after that, Porter would pull happily to greet Roger when they saw him on the trail. "Roger would always ask, 'Is this normal? What does it mean?' And I would say, 'It's not really normal, but it means he likes you.'" On the bike trail where stimulations can be high, Susan says that seeing Roger has a calming effect on Porter.

Porter's acceptance of Roger hasn't just been a pleasantry

exchanged on the bike trail; he has become a precious friend to Susan.

Jim Green

Jim, or "Dr. Green," as Susan calls him, is a historian, a professor in the School of Education at Mount St. Joseph, and one of Porter's people that Susan most wanted me to meet. And while I did see him on the trail once when I walked with Susan and Porter, it wasn't until the cookout Susan hosted, at which I read an excerpt of the book, that I connected with him more. Not only had he visited the bike trail thinking he had missed the book-signing event for this book, but he and his family drove the entire day to make it to Susan's cookout and my reading. Such thoughtfulness! No wonder Porter had accepted him, although Jim says it was actually his daughter Meredith that Porter took to first.

"One of the first times we saw Susan and Porter on the trail, Meredith got down on her knees and Porter came to her," says Jim. "It took some time, after that, of talking with Susan on other occasions, for him to warm to me." Jim says he talked with Susan at length about Porter, and eventually Porter would allow him to hold the leash. "He's such a noble animal. It's amazing how Susan has taken care of him. It's a gift."

Jason

Jason is the general manager of properties for the Dan Beard Council Boy Scouts. When I first met him, I thought he could be anyone's neighbor, because he reminded me of so many of my dad's friends that would pull in the driveway to say hello when I was a kid—he's a family man, and his good-naturedness puts you at ease. But there's also a seriousness about him. Trustworthy is the overall descriptor that comes to mind, and perhaps that's what Porter sees in him.

As he's still considered the ranger for the local Boy Scout woods, where Susan often walks Porter, Jason grants permission, on an individual basis and only when camp is not in session, for local people to walk their dogs and hike on the property.

It was on these walks that Jason gradually got to know Susan and Porter. "Porter wanted absolutely nothing to do with me at first. He cowered behind Colin and Susan the first several times. I think it started to change when my kids started coming over; he started to let me in a little closer. I'd see them when I sat out on the picnic table having my morning coffee."

Jason's son Wyatt loves to see "the wolfdog lady" with Porter, which he often does when his mom brings him to the entrance to the Boy Scout property to wait for the school bus each morning.

"He's a gentle giant, and a lot of people don't know that," Jason continues. "If you don't know him, people assume the worst, that he'll be aggressive. I still have to remind the kids that he doesn't like them getting in his face and that they have to respect boundaries that aren't necessarily there with other dogs. Still, it's miraculous to see how far he's come from where he's been."

Mike, Eleni, and Jim of Mike's Mobile Veterinary Services

Susan has often said that Porter's story—and essentially his life—really begins with these folks. Although I never got to meet Jim the vet tech, or to see the incredible mobile truck with which they serve the Greater Cincinnati area as veterinarians, I remember the day that Mike and Eleni came out to Susan's house to meet me. The gesture was clearly reflective of the generosity and kindness that motivated their efforts to rescue Porter and to continue to provide care for him once Susan had adopted him.

After Porter's rescue in December of 2013, not only did Mike's Mobile become the family vet for all of Susan and Colin's dogs (three at the time, and one has since passed away), but Eleni says she spoke with Susan often for the first year Porter was with them.

Mike and his wife Eleni, along with their vet techs, have taken a great deal of special care in meeting Porter's veterinary needs. Their first visit to Porter's new home was to neuter him. He had to be mildly sedated and muzzled in order to get him into the van where the surgery would be performed. At the time, Porter was not comfortable with Mike at all, and their first vet tech, Robin, was in attendance.

Mike's Mobile stepped up when a serious health issue arose for Porter. He developed a sarcoma, a classification based on the layer of skin it inhabits. The cause was unknown. It required three surgeries, in October of 2015, July of 2016, and October of 2017. The first occurrence just appeared to be a fatty tumor. The second was a different color and shape, and the third was completely different—gray fluids were present and not well encapsulated. In the "debulking" surgery, as Mike refers to it, he was not able to get all of it, and not equipped in the truck to do the necessary radiation. "Think of it like roots of a tree," Mike says of what remained of the sarcoma. "They are there, but they are microscopic."

It eventually became necessary for Susan to seek more advanced veterinary care, beyond what Mike's Mobile could accomplish with their equipment. But they remain dedicated in their service to Colin and Susan, and fond of Porter.

The second vet tech, Jim, first saw Porter in February of 2015. He was off the chain by then. "All of us were thrilled to watch Porter's progress off the chain and in his enclosure," says Eleni, although she is typically not in attendance on appointments with Mike and Jim. Porter had gotten more comfortable with Robin "and it's gotten a lot better with Jim," confirms Mike. "We're still cautious—we take all precautions. Jim will put Porter in lock position so that he can't turn and bite during treatment."

Jim's warm, open smile and carefree appearance are certainly reflective of his success in handling Porter. Susan describes how fearless he has been. "From the beginning, he has just gotten right in there with Porter, even putting his arms around Porter, which Porter would not normally tolerate from a man, given his history."

He seemed to have a good rapport with Porter from the outset and has been fearless during Porter's visits. "I only feel confidence with him," says Jim. "I always enter any situation with an animal with intention—I'm confident and happy and pleasant; never fear or doubts with Porter. I think animals can sense people better than people can sense people."

He describes Porter as being nervous but not aggressive. "You always use caution," he warns, and goes on to explain that as the tech, he's the one with his hands on Porter first, and expressing affection, versus Mike, who, as the vet, is the one examining, poking, and administering shots and other treatments. For this reason, Porter senses Mike differently, which may be why Porter is still not completely comfortable with him. "His trust in me has increased," though, Mike says. "He comes into the truck more willingly, and he's not as nervous. I'd like to be closer to him, but as a patient, his trust in me has improved. He's come a long way."

On being part of Porter's rescue, Mike says, "When I think how he could have been dead if another vet had been called and agreed to euthanize him, we would have missed this opportunity. Every time we see him, I'm reminded that we helped save a life and create a happy environment. It's priceless."

Eleni, who has kind eyes and a gentle demeanor, speaks candidly and fondly of her relationship with Porter.

"I will always be in awe of Porter at how much he's overcome, and he still wants to learn. He is so smart, and I do believe he knew we were there that day to change his life for the better," says Eleni, who adds that she had her own issues to work through regarding Porter. "I had to rid myself of the false sense of responsibility [when it came to his rescue]. I also had to forgive his former owner. Initially I was very upset and that increased the fear in my thinking. I am always glad to see Porter and there's a mutual respect. I'm thrilled he had a happy ending!"

Eleni says that Porter and his rescue inspired her to start her own trap, neuter, release (TNR) cat rescue, which includes monitoring of several outdoor feline colonies, and facilitation of foster homes and adoptions. "I love trapping and seeing a colony decreased by lack of kittens. I love seeing cats I trapped months ago become healthy because they received the help they needed. We are also huge believers in education and telling others about the importance of TNR and how it benefits the cats and surrounding communities."

Mike's Mobile has had several patients who are hybrids (a term that is still used outside of the wolfdog community), and they perform all services, including surgeries and vaccinations.

Ohio State University and Blue Buffalo Foundation

When the cancer returned for a fourth time, Susan seemed to be out of options for Porter, with Mike's Mobile Vet having done all they could and no other vet in the city willing to see a wolfdog like Porter at the time. "They called him wildlife and wouldn't even talk to me," says Susan. So she went out on a limb and contacted a running friend, Dr. Juli Goldstein, an aquatic veterinary consultant and motivational speaker who played herself in the movie *Dolphin Tale 2*.

"I just took a chance, because if anyone would have an idea about who could help me, or a connection to someone who would, she would, since she had done this amazing work with the dolphin, and had gone through cancer treatment for her own dog," Susan says.

It was this inquiry that ultimately paid off. Dr. Goldstein told Susan about groundbreaking work in oncology that was taking place at Ohio State University. The Hummel & Truman Hospital for Companion Animals at the OSU Veterinary Medical Center was where she and Porter finally found help. But there was no golden ticket—Susan was also initially turned down there as well, because, Susan explains, OSU is a learning institution and they classified Porter as "wildlife." She credits a vet tech named Mat with convincing those in authority at the hospital to take the case, but it's also not clear exactly what the deciding factor was in OSU agreeing to treat Porter.

"He kept calling me back and asking me for more details, more information and vet reports and photos of the tumor. I don't know who Mat was having to check with, but it took about three days for them to agree to see him," says Susan, but

113

she confirms that "all of the doctors were fantastic."

However, Dr. Bertran, who performed the surgery, said that "It was definitely a good story," because Porter and Susan have a special connection. "I wanted to give him every single opportunity to be comfortable and hopefully give them more days together. When Susan contacted our surgical oncology service at Ohio State University, Matty was the person who gave me the message in regard to Porter and his recurrent issue. This type of tumor is usually responsive to surgical excision, and that was my whole goal. Trying to see what surgical option could be best for him, as well as trying to help him to feel better and help Susan to have his companionship for longer. Those were the two main goals, but when we treat the type of cancer, as a surgeon, I want to be aggressive because we know we can achieve a potential cure." There was one consultation, and the surgery, an all-day procedure, was scheduled for the following day, with extensive prep beforehand and significant time for Porter to come out of the anesthesia.

Dr. Bertran sheds more light on the whole process. "The first thing that we did was to get Porter into the clinic, firstly to meet him and Susan and secondly to do a CT scan in order to plan what surgical options we had. That first day was a success, we felt that Porter liked us, and I always felt really part of the team with Susan. She knows Porter amazingly well, and she was always letting us know when she felt that Porter was happy or nervous. She was always very accommodating to our protocols but at the same time we accommodated them, to make their experience in a stressful environment like the hospital much better. Once we had a CT scan, and the options laid down for Susan, we decided to be as aggressive as we could with the surgical excision, planning on combining our surgery with radiation therapy."

The logistics of transporting Porter from Cincinnati to Columbus, not only for the surgery itself but for the preliminary visits and follow-up radiation treatments, had to be ironed out, as well as the particular on-site protocols for treating a wolfdog.

Since Porter becomes very agitated and uncomfortable on car rides of any significant length, two sedatives were to be administered before each trip with no food. Several of these trips proved to be a challenge.

One journey was made in the driving rain of a severe storm. Susan got lost, which made her late. Both she and Porter were agitated, but the OSU client liaison, Genie, talked her through getting back on the right route to get to the clinic.

In a different instance, Susan had forgotten and given Porter food with the sedative. She called en route to report this and was forced to turn around when they couldn't do the treatment for fear that Porter could vomit or gag while under anesthesia.

Upon arrival at the animal hospital, Porter would be taken in by a back entrance in order to avoid other animals in the main lobby. Susan describes how the lighting was dimmed in the exam rooms for him. Following treatments, he was wheeled straight out to Susan's car, where he would wake up on the ride home.

Even with everything in place for Porter's treatment, the cost remained prohibitive. Much to Susan's relief, Dr. Bertran, along with Genie, delivered the good news that Susan and Porter would be the recipients of a grant from the Blue Buffalo Foundation, which paid for the surgery and allowed the family to afford the cost of the radiation treatments. "This was an incredibly gracious and most unexpected surprise," says Susan. "We knew nothing about the Blue Buffalo Foundation, but learned that they work with six research institutions in the US, offering grant money for cancer research."

Along with the rest of the team there, Susan also speaks highly of Genie as being "another favorite OSU person." As a client liaison, Genie handles paperwork and logistics. "I also try to be an advocate for both the client and the patient in terms of navigating the oncological process," says Genie. "Porter came to see us when I was fairly new to my position. I had the opportunity to follow the case through surgery. It was an honor and truly a privilege to be a part of Porter's team and ensure that his appointments went as smoothly as possible for both patient and client. The family's dedication to his health and well-being was—and is—inspiring. Their gratitude for his care and the experience will remain with me always."

With the tumor removed in totality, attention turned to Porter's follow-up radiation treatment. Again, his unique circumstances had to be taken into consideration. Porter's difficulty traveling in the car made the daily recommended doses of 3Gy radiation problematic. Instead, four higher doses (8Gy) were given once a week over four weeks.

This experience was stressful and arduous for all concerned. But the staff of the OSU clinic, and the philanthropic efforts of Blue Buffalo, were with Susan and Porter throughout.

Fred

It goes without saying that Fred has been a crucial and integral part of Porter's recovery from the treatment he received from his former owner. And while he really credits Susan with Porter's success with the training, he is certainly among those whom Porter has accepted into his circle, and in addition to being the trainer with the expertise that Susan and Porter needed, he has become a valuable friend to them.

I was a little nervous to meet him for the first time, and wondered if I would measure up, as the person writing Porter's story. But Fred is easy to talk to, and even easier to listen to—though I haven't gotten to work with Fred as a trainer, or witnessed him working, I loved getting to know him through his stories, of which there are many. When I asked him about his experience working with protection dogs, rather than listing bullet points of his resume, he leaned in and said "Here's what you want to know," before he told me about his work with the German shepherd at the K9 security unit that no other staff member could, or would handle.

It wasn't until the second time I saw Fred, that I, along with my husband Andrew, got to meet his pack: his German shepherd Rose (the very same he'd used in the protection exercise with Susan), a female shepherd-wolf mix named Sky, and a Doberman named Rocko. These three animals are an even better testament to Fred's expertise than his stories. When Andy and I entered his office (since Fred is the co-owner of the establishment, every day can be bring-your-pack-to-work day), they remained seated on the floor until Fred said "Ok, go say hello," and they came over to greet us. I think Rose sniffed me the longest, which didn't surprise me. I fell in love with Sky, who came near me several times during the visit. And Rocko, Fred would agree, was the clown of the group—he was always the last to comply with Fred's commands, and at one point Fred spoke to him in German. "I can have one or more of them sitting under my desk at my feet and no one would know it," says Fred. When he's on the grounds of his workplace alone, he can let them out to roam, and bring them back with one whistle. He was clearly the right man for the job when it came to Susan and Porter.

He speaks with a matter-of-fact candor about his relationship with Porter. "He always comes to me. Anytime she's ever brought him around me, he's always let me pet him. Our relationship is one of respect."

Dale

Dale, like most of Porter's other people, is close to Susan and Colin and to Susan in particular. She says "he's like a brother to me." Susan and her family used to be Dale's neighbors, and as the owner of Eads Fence, he answered the call to build Porter's enclosure without question.

However, there is one big difference between Dale and

Porter's other people—Porter has not accepted Dale into his pack. In fact, Dale's presence agitates Porter to such a degree that when Susan is walking him on the bike trail, Porter will go on high alert when he senses Dale approaching, which he can do long before Susan ever sees Dale coming. Porter's hackles can get up, and he huffs and growls as he backs away from Dale.

No one has been able to pinpoint the reason for Porter's rejection of Dale, although it's entirely possible that Dale reminds Porter of his first owner in some way. According to Fred, it could be as simple as Dale using the same deodorant or aftershave as the other man.

And while it continues to be a point of frustration and disappointment for Susan and Dale that one of her dearest friends has not been accepted by Porter, this challenge does not negate the fact that Dale is responsible for building Porter's enclosure, without which Porter would still need to be kept on the chain. Dale has provided the safety through which Porter could become socialized and participate in the ever-expanding opportunities that await him off the chain. Without a doubt, Dale is one of Porter's people, even if Porter himself is not yet comfortable with that.

I first met Dale when he came to Susan's house to have lunch with us in April of 2019. His kindness and affection for

Susan showed in his warm smile. I, too, wondered how it was possible that Porter could have such an aversion to him.

After lunch, we all went out to Porter's enclosure. At first Dale stood right next to Susan, very close to the fence. Porter approached, took a treat from Susan, and sniffed Dale's hand. Then it was like someone flipped a switch that caused Porter to remember that he didn't like Dale at all. He backed away from the fence and began huffing and growling. He paced within the enclosure, and no matter what end Dale was outside of the fence, Porter would move to the opposite end inside his enclosure.

But once Susan and Dale moved some distance away from the enclosure, Porter sat down and was completely calm. Some might not call this a victory, but the entire exchange was much less dramatic than some of Porter's reactions to Dale on the bike trail.

With time and continued patience on all sides, there is no limit to how Porter's relationships with people and other animals can expand. It does seem clear that these relationships evolve in Porter's own time and based on his comfort level.

Dale's motivation for taking the job to build the enclosure is definitely rooted in his friendship with Susan. "She's a best friend and I will do most anything that is for her and her family's greater good." He also says that he saw the job as providing Susan with a way to "safely and responsibly contain a beautiful animal and to protect it from harm's way."

"He's beautiful, like wild animals are, but he has kind manners as Sue leads him around on his leash. I think of all the people that see him on the bike trail, their expressions and their emotions. I think of how all those same people's lives are affected for just that moment by interacting with Porter and Sue," concludes Dale. "Porter has a spirit that attracts people to him. He stands strong and confident and creates an emotion that's not easy to describe."

Undoubtedly that emotion reflects a desire and a readiness to continue to be available to Porter, should he ever decide to recognize Dale as a member of his pack.

Susan

I don't believe that Susan ended up with Porter by accident. There are perhaps others who could have given a safe home to Porter—people with the financial resources, along with the property and means to build him an enclosure—people who could check off the list of requirements of his care. But I believe that Susan and Colin were the *right* people to adopt Porter, and she has definitely been the right person to have overcome all of Porter's challenges with him. Her selfless devotion has carried both of them through all manner of trials—I can only add what I have seen and experienced of her as both the author and her friend.

Susan has been a lovely and kind friend to me since I've known her, but my visits to Ohio have made us close. Susan expresses a profound generosity of a magnitude that is rare these days. The passion she demonstrates for the wellbeing of animals extends to the people who are lucky enough to find themselves in her orbit. When you're with her, you won't be allowed to be cold or hungry for long. If sadness or distress has darkened your day, it won't last in her presence; she melts it with her kindness, and with the joy and laughter that inevitably accompany the warmth of her smile and the twinkle in her eyes.

This story makes it pretty clear how she feels about Porter, but her own words on their relationship still speak volumes: "No animal has had my attention or heart quite like Porter, except my first dog, a little black gnarly terrier mix named Willard. Porter is special. Because he is so high-maintenance and lives outside, I spend a great deal of time with him, walking him, taking him places, trying to acclimate him to the house, to get him time out of the enclosure. Early on, fear, and anxiety, were a large part of my relationship with him. But as we grew to understand each other, and I knew what his behaviors meant and could read his body language, I relaxed, he then relaxed, and we have really bonded since then. I like to wonder how many miles we have walked together in our almost six years. It's thousands and thousands, for sure!"

And while I can't ask Porter for his comments on her, she has told me how he'll stop when they are walking and just look up at her; how, when they first started walking with other wolfdogs, he would look to her for reassurance that they were in a good place; how their bond becomes stronger with every trial and its resulting victory. Porter is Susan's, and she is his. Love abounds. Enough said.

Meeting Porter

I made this the final chapter of the book so that the reader (unless you skipped ahead) would have the benefit of seeing all that Porter had come through, and how he'd grown and overcome so much by the time I first met him. I had no idea how profoundly I would be touched by meeting him, and what an impact doing this project would have on me as a writer.

Susan has said to me more than once that Porter brought me back to her and Colin. Not only that, but he brought me back to my hometown, a place that did not hold happy adult memories for me, and to other dear friends there whom I really had no expectation of seeing anytime soon, since I hadn't planned on returning after I closed up my dad's house in 1997.

But one day, as I sat at the Ugly Mug coffee shop in Burbank, I found myself posting a flyer on Facebook of my editorial services that I had created for the graduate course I was taking at the time. Very quickly, a comment from Susan appeared on the post: "You should write Porter's story!" I dismissed it at first, and replied that it was her story to tell, but that I could certainly help her edit it. Thank goodness, some universal hand thwacked me on the back of the head. What was wrong with me? I have loved Porter since I saw the first picture Susan shared of him on Facebook. I had followed his story through his ups and downs, and my first feeling upon seeing his photos was similar to Gwen's when she saw Susan walking him in their neighborhood: "I have to meet this big beautiful boy!" On almost every Facebook post of Susan's I would make a comment about how I wanted to meet him, and she would comment back that their guesthouse was waiting for me, and so was Porter. Now was my chance.

But I had this idea that it would take huge amounts of time and money just to get started. But when I took a closer look at my situation, I had a week's vacation and an unused airline ticket. I coordinated with Susan, and less than two days later, I had my vacation approved. Within a week I had my plane ticket.

"Someday" finally came in the fall of 2018. I spent a lot of time preparing for my journey to meet Porter, both practically and spiritually. After twenty years away from my hometown, I found myself in their living room on a warm October day, stitching together the highlights of our lives. After a while, we headed outside to Porter's enclosure. It was time.

Having talked to Susan at length about the protocol for

meeting Porter, I knew there were only a few possibilities for the outcome. One extreme was that he would immediately feel uncomfortable with me for whatever reason, and make it known—in other words, he'd want nothing to do with me. A second response is one that many people get from him, which is a sniff, and perhaps the chance to give him a treat. But then he'll move away. This is tolerance without a desire for extended interaction.

The other extreme is full acceptance. When this happens Porter will give a "lean-in" or a "curl-in"—that "wolfie hug," as I like to call it—in which he puts his scent on you. This is the golden ticket into his pack.

Of course, my heart wanted acceptance. But more than that, I just wanted him to feel unconditional love from me, free of any expectations. I told Susan that I would love him and be with him on his terms. She said that she felt certain he would accept me, but that it might take some time, as it usually does. I decided that even if he never fully accepted me, just getting to meet him in person was a gift I would always treasure.

Susan gave me a couple of treats to hold in my hand. I stood several feet back from his enclosure, already in awe. She brought him out on his lead (he is never outside of his enclosure without it) and led him over to me. I stood perfectly still while he sniffed me and of course took the treats out of my hand (was I going to stop him?).

And then it happened. He curled into me. I had won the great gift of his acceptance. Susan told me that he'd never done that on a first meeting before. And from there it only got better.

When Porter shows affection, he's intentional and specific with it. Shortly after I got my lean-in that day, he sat in front of me and looked up at me. I'd always been taught not to look any animal, especially dogs, directly in the eye, since it can be perceived as a challenge. But Susan told me that when he's looking at me, I need to look back at him, because he's showing affection. It's true, because when I did look into his eyes, I felt bathed in warmth, trust, joy, and love.

Later in the week during that first visit, I had the privilege of not only going inside his enclosure, but sitting on his platform, which is a huge honor. I was rewarded with nips (very light nibbles, another way wolves show affection) and licks all over.

While Fred says that Porter responded positively because I "did everything I was supposed to do," meaning I followed protocol by standing still with my hands at my side and let him come to me, Susan and I both feel that something spiritual took place in that moment.

Some have asked me if I was afraid. I can honestly say

that I was never for one moment afraid of Porter, not in the way that people think. Knowing how intelligent he is, I was afraid he would sense my flaws, and all that I struggle with, and would not want me in his circle, much less in his pack. Fred also said that Porter accepts people because he sees something in them that he needs, or he has something to give that they need. Meeting him was incredible.

When I returned home after that first visit, I was so full of the joy of the experience, yet I felt at a loss to convey it all to my husband Andrew. I could only tell him about it and hope that he could have his own experience at some point. He asked many questions about Porter's behavior. He also hoped that he would be accepted by Porter as I was.

He got his chance when we returned to Ohio together in January. It ended up being a special visit in which not only did he bond with Porter, but Susan and Colin included him in their family just as they had done with me—my friendship with them was now his, and the circle was complete. Andrew also bonded with Jelena over their shared love of music and singing, and they spent several hours at the piano together.

I had already received my welcome when I'd arrived the evening before, and Colin and Susan and I went for a walk in the woods that border their property. We took their other two dogs as well, and there was a lot of commotion at the outset, because not only had Susan not seen Porter all day, her schedule having prevented her from getting Porter his normal morning walk, but Colin was there along with their two dogs, Sweetie and Scout—not to mention me. My initial greeting was a bit frenetic and I wondered if he truly remembered me.

But once we got deep into the woods, we stopped to sit on a bench that had been placed there. Porter jumped on the bench between Susan and me, and I received my nips and kisses. I was home.

The following evening, I returned from the airport well after dark with Andrew. The first order of business was to have dinner, after which it was finally Andrew's turn to meet Porter. He and I had talked at length before this trip, and his approach was much the same as mine had been. He just wanted Porter to feel love, and while he very much hoped to be accepted fully by him, Andrew would love and respect Porter on Porter's terms rather than his own.

Susan turned on the floodlight at the side of the house near the dog enclosures and brought Porter out on the lead. Andrew and I thought it might help if we held hands, to show Porter not only that Andrew was a safe person for him, but that he was, in essence, with me. There were a few tentative sniffs and then Porter backed away.

Susan said, "Let's walk."

The easiest way to make Porter comfortable with anyone is to have him walk with them. In this way, Colin and Susan themselves earned Porter's trust, as wells as their kids and other two dogs, became integrated into Porter's pack. We all took off together, Colin with Sweetie and Scout, Susan with Porter, and Andrew and me bringing up the rear.

At the end of the walk that night, Andrew knelt down next to Porter and received a few kisses. Susan reiterates that this was the most acceptance Porter had ever given any *man* on a first greeting. We were excited and grateful.

The next morning, we ventured into a different part of the woods to a historical gravesite, and once again we had Colin and the other dogs with us. We were all talking about the history of the site, and suddenly Porter curled into Andrew and gifted him a wolf hug. Once again this was a record for a man—full acceptance within two days.

Fred had told both Susan and me that every person's relationship with Porter is different. He very much loves both Andrew and me, but I noticed that Porter makes different sounds, almost the same guttural noises of approval he makes for Sweetie and Scout, when he's greeting Andrew.

It was wonderful to see Porter in his magnificent full winter coat. Andy and I mused that there we were, just walking through the snowy woods in the dead of night with "our" wolf.

Our precious few days there together went quickly. On one of our last mornings with Porter, we walked with him and Susan in a snowy field. As she romped with him, something happened—for a brief moment, it seemed as if I watched the flickering scene of a home movie. In that moment I saw Porter not with my eyes but with my understanding. Time stopped. The vastness of life and love he expresses rushed through me.

As we walked back to the house, Porter did something he's done often with Susan. He turned and stood in front of me and Andrew. He looked up at us and curled in, scenting us with his body heavily and intentionally across both pairs of our legs. He repeated this several times before we left the field and entered their driveway on the main road. Without words, he communicated his definitive love for us. With tears in my eyes again, I told Susan that I would never forget those moments.

It seems that I can't stay away for more than a couple of months at a time. I was soon planning my next trip, unfortunately without Andrew this time, for April of that year. This visit was special in many ways, including my time with Susan, in which our friendship deepened. It was also a more relaxed visit for me, with not so many activities planned. I enjoyed an entire afternoon of writing this book in the idyll of their home surrounded by the beauty of springtime.

My bond with Porter became deeper and more special as well, if that's even possible. When I first arrived, Susan called me just as I was exiting the freeway near their house. She ran to get him out of his enclosure so that they would be in the driveway to greet me. In spite of delays with both my connecting flight and my rental car, I still pulled in just before dusk, so I could see him in daylight.

Susan was waiting with him by the pond in their front yard. I stopped the car a good length up from the house and got out. I bent down and slapped my hands on my knees, which got Porter to fairly drag Susan, who held on to his leash for dear life, down the driveway to greet me. He nipped at every part of me he could reach and gave me licks. It was one of the best homecomings I have had. Because it's like that—every time I pull into their driveway, it's like coming home. And every time I go, I leave a huge piece of my heart behind for him, for Susan, for all of them.

On other visits I had stayed in their guesthouse at the other end of the driveway. This time, I stayed in a room in their basement that looked right out at Porter and the girls. One night as I lay there, the full moon shone in through the window. With Porter just outside, it was heaven.

On my first morning there, I had heard sirens, but I thought they signified the second Friday of the month, or something equally innocuous. In fact, there was a tornado warning in effect. I stayed in bed for a while after the sirens ceased and opened the doors to my room to see that Susan had brought Porter into his indoor kennel because of the weather warnings.

It felt like Christmas morning. For a brief few minutes, Susan allowed him out of the kennel off-leash. He ran to me, skittering slightly on the tile floor of the basement. More kisses and more nips. Susan and I sat down on the floor and he lay between us for a few moments while we talked and stroked his fur.

Whenever I leave Ohio, I carry Porter with me in many ways—myriad photos of a thousand moments with him; a locket containing one such photo, a gift from Susan, worn close to my heart; a sandwich bag filled with huge tufts of the winter coat he shed in the warmth of April.

I make a game of pulling my sweatshirt out of its own bag to present it to my cats. It is its own animal to them, strange and wild. Before I surrender it to the washing machine, I lift it again to my nose and inhale the earth and wind and sky of that winter day in the field, the musky signature he scented us with that fills his enclosure where I sat on his platform next to him for last nips and nuzzles before we left, all that I carry home in my heart's memory.

Porter's acceptance and love remain among the best gifts I will ever receive. I treasure every moment spent with him and Susan. I love being her "wingman" when we walk on the bike trail together. There is nothing better than reaching down and resting my fingers in Porter's thick fur. It has been my immense pleasure and privilege to write this book, and I hope that it will give readers at least some small glimpse of Porter's magnificence and the miracle of his story.

Epilogue: A New Pack

As of the writing of this book, Porter's horizons continue to widen, and his experiences in the world continue to expand. On one of her walks with Porter on the bike trail, Susan encountered a woman named Nikki, who, along with her husband, is part of Ohio River Wolves, a closed group of dog and wolfdog owners that hike with their animals on a regular basis.

After talking with her for a few minutes, Susan discovered that Nikki's dog, Rama, was a wolfdog. Nikki had already heard about Porter from others on the bike trail who knew about him. She extended an invitation to Susan and Porter to join them, and the following week Susan did just that.

On this first experience with the group, after a stressful car ride, Porter had his hackles up, snarling, huffing, and lunging as the other wolf dogs arrived. But the group waited patiently for him to become calm, and after about ten minutes, Porter quieted down and they were able to follow the group at a distance. Nikki reassured Susan that Porter just doesn't know how to engage.

When Porter would watch the other dogs, their play would trigger aggression in him. It's Porter's opportunity to learn to be with and interact with his peers.

Andra, another member of the group, and her arctic wolfdog, Tiamat, were among the first to make overtures to greet and interact with Porter. On the first attempt, Porter and Tiamat surprisingly touched noses. Susan describes Tiamat as a sweet, submissive animal who was interested in Porter. But after only a couple of seconds, Porter lunged, and she cowered.

The second time Susan and Porter hiked with the group, her son, JC, was also with them. Porter still behaved aggressively as the other wolfdogs gathered, but Susan was able to follow the group more closely than before. A second attempt was made to interact with Tiamat, but Porter became snappy as she approached, so the mission was aborted.

Their third hike with the group, which included Susan's nephew and his wife, was a rainy, muddy affair on a narrow trail. Susan was able to lead Porter closer than on the previous two hikes, but an individual with a dog, who was not part of the group, ran by them on the narrow trail, crowding them out. In his agitation at the close-range disruption in his space, Porter lunged at Rama, causing Nikki herself to slide in the mud. All ended well, however, and Nikki described the incident as one of misplaced aggression on Porter's part. "That is how awesome and supportive they are," exclaims Susan, who describes their fourth walk with the group as "by far the most satisfying."

While Porter still wasn't entirely comfortable getting face to face with any of the other animals, he at last felt relaxed enough to walk next to them and even lie down near them. Though he would give a snap or a snarl when another dog would get too close for his comfort level, Nikki and the others deemed the behavior normal for a wolfdog, who communicate differently than other dogs. "He is actually being polite," she told Susan, "and telling them what he is comfortable with and what he isn't comfortable with."

As for Tiamat, she and Porter were finally able to sit side by side and were begging treats from one of the members of the group. At one point shortly after, she sat with her back to Porter, who sniffed her backside. This would be quite rude for humans on their third or fourth date, but is considered a "getting to know you" gesture in the dog world. Tiamat allowed it, but when she turned her head to look at him, he snapped and snarled. This fourth hike, however, "gave me hope," says Susan. "I am so grateful to have met Nikki and to have been invited to join this wolf group on walks. They are so understanding and supportive."

These milestones of behavioral progress are evidence that Porter, who Susan says would constantly look up at her for reassurance during these hikes, is beginning to understand that no harm will come to him or Susan as a result of these adventures. Nothing will be taken from him, and he only has everything to gain. "We are peeling back the layers and expanding his life experiences," says Susan. "And it's precious."

Chained. Waiting for food, for life, for love. Hit, chained, waiting, surviving. Three thousand sunsets. Countless clouds. Hurtling toward a hard stop. One hand with a heart ended that plot. Unchained: a sniff, a nip, a breath. A walk, and back again, a run, and back again into safety, warmth, nourishment, love. Venturing out and returning home on a path apart, a circle of trust, gathering tentative greetings, one more, two more, on the way back home. Forward, and double back, looking up with eyes that love and receive love, curling in, even to sit at a stranger's feet at last. A sniff, a breath. A ripple on the water, a footprint in the snow. The circle widens.

Suggested Further Reading and Resources

Websites and Social Media:
Full Moon Farm – fullmoonfarm.org
Gray Wolf Conservation – graywolfconservation.com
Nicole Wilde – nicolewilde.com
Southern Ohio Wolf Sanctuary –
        southernohiowolfsanctuary.com
Texas Wolfdog Project – texaswolfdogproject.org
The Bark – https://thebark.com/content/do-wolfdogs-make-
        good-pets
Wolf Love and Education Facebook group
World of Lupines Foundation (W.O.L.F) Facebook page

Articles:
"Can Idaho Wolves Shed Their 'Big Bad' Reputation?"
        https://www.csmonitor.com/Environment/2018/1025/
        Can-Idaho-wolves-shed-their-big-bad-
        reputation?cmpid=shared-email
"Is Your 'Wolf-Dog' Really a Wolf-Dog? How to Tell" –
        https://windstoneeditions.com/forums/topic/is-your-
        wolf-dog-really-a-wolf-dog-how-to-tell/

Books:
Kinship with All Life, by J. Allen Boone
Letters to Strongheart, by J. Allen Boone
*Wolf, Spirit of the Wild: A Celebration of Wolves in Word and
        Image* by Diana Landau (editor)

Made in the
USA
Lexington, KY